MILLER AND MIDDLE AMERICA

Essays on Arthur Miller
and the American Experience

Edited by

Paula T. Langteau

University Press of America,® Inc.
Lanham · Boulder · New York · Toronto · Plymouth, UK

Copyright © 2007 by
University Press of America,® Inc.
4501 Forbes Boulevard
Suite 200
Lanham, Maryland 20706
UPA Acquisitions Department (301) 459-3366

Estover Road
Plymouth PL6 7PY
United Kingdom

Library of Congress Control Number: 2006941019
ISBN-13: 978-0-7618-3710-7 (paperback : alk. paper)
ISBN-10: 0-7618-3710-8 (paperback : alk. paper)

To my husband, Leo,
and my children,
Nicholas and Galen,
whose love and unwavering support
mean everything

Contents

Preface

In 1970, with nine plays to Arthur Miller's credit, Harold Clurman wrote, "There can be no doubt at this point in our literary and theatrical history as to Arthur Miller's position in it" (vii). Twenty-five years later, by which time Miller had written twenty-four, Christopher Bigsby recognized, "The range and impact of his work is such that today no living playwright could be said to be his equal. Not a day passes without a production of a Miller play somewhere in the world" (x). At the time of Bigsby's writing, commenting on the six-decade span between the 1930s, when Miller started writing plays, and the 1990s, Bigsby reflected: "In those sixty years, he has engaged in a debate with America and its values, and staged the struggle of men and women anxious to understand their lives and to insist on their significance.... Miller has written plays in every decade of this century since the 1930s. They add up to an alternative history of a troubled century" (xxv).

As we entered the 21st century, Arthur Miller stood as the single greatest living American playwright, still writing, still serving, at age 88, as "a chronicler of American culture, which he has both characterized and criticized" (Otten ix). Michael Billington said of Miller, "He remains totally anchored in American life while challenging almost all of the values and beliefs that make the society tick. He is the late twentieth century's most eloquent critic of the devalued American dream" (189).

Recognizing Miller's monumental contribution to the literary life of America, the contributors to this collection gathered in Wisconsin for the Eighth International Arthur Miller Conference in late October of 2003 to share their scholarship, focusing on the theme of "Miller and Middle America." The playwright, struggling with failing health, could not attend. Assembled quite literally in the middle of America, we spoke about what makes Miller's work uniquely American, what elements of his writing represent the institutions we hold sacred and the very land on which we walk, and what meaning we can draw from Miller's intense investigation of these factors that interplay with our understanding of ourselves to help shape who we are. The essays in this collection represent a compilation of the scholarship we shared.

Steven Centola's "Arthur Miller: Guardian of the Dream of America" served as the conference's closing keynote address but here serves well to set the framework for the essays in this volume. In it, he describes the historical role of literary artists in America, from Puritan times through the present, "wrestl[ing] with their own confusion about what it meant to be an American, what burden and obligation, what privileges and benefits, what traditions and inheritances, what myths and contradictions awaited them in their own personal exploration of the society and culture that surrounded and enveloped them" (5). While much in our literary history celebrates our culture, the artist must also grapple with our shortcomings. Centola calls this

> the central role—the crucial, inevitable, and pivotal role—for the literary artist in free society: to serve as the voice of the people who are silenced by fear and intolerance; to ask the challenging and difficult questions of a government, a society, a people that prefer self-congratulatory praise to unflinching moral self-scrutiny; to be the conscience of a nation that finds it uncomfortable to undergo the rigorous examination of the dark recesses of the national psyche and individual soul that earnest and self-evaluation necessitate. (2)

Certainly, throughout his career, Miller did not shy away from this responsibility; he embraced it, recognizing, as Centola points out, that "art not only derives from life experience, but it must also respond to life and improve the conditions of life and living for humanity" (3). And Miller *did* respond. Not only do his writings demonstrate that he understood American history and values but "Miller's historical vision is enlarged by his remarkable ability to synthesize past and present circumstance and to find in the immediate events a corresponding analogue whose example is instructive and perhaps even curative to a national psyche fractured by its own internal contradictions" (Centola 7).

Throughout American history, we have often distorted or simply "erased" the truth of injustice in favor of promoting "a national mythology that celebrates the ideals of diversity and freedom." When that happens, playwrights like Miller remind us that our "beginnings are never quite as good as the myth implies," writes Lewis Livesay, in "Hegemony, Hatred and the Scapegoat Mechanism" (15). Livesay explores how *"Playing for Time* and *The Crucible* feature totalitarian attempts to impose a purified homogeneity upon society" (17). Livesay starts with an examination of the oedipal conflict that arises naturally in humans following a perceived threat to the infant symbiotic relationship with the mother, and then describes how in religion and "in facism, we discern the attempt to return to a maternal-like absorption through immersion in a group feverishly united to share a common dream" (18). But, the social restraint that keeps the oedipal urge in check, learned as we mature, lessens in a group setting, more readily turning into aggression. Livesay describes how *"The Crucible* and *Playing for Time* both reveal how repressed aggression can reemerge as hemegonic totalitarianism sanctioning murder" (19). The tale is cautionary: "Evil is not just Hitler or Puritanical judges or McCarthy; evil is human. It is endemic to the process of trying to live together. It can be restrained, but never eliminated. It can rear its ugly head in Salem, in Wisconsin, in Washington, in Europe—anywhere and everywhere" (Livesay 21).

Like in Livesay's analysis, with "An Interrogation of Middle American Political Correctness," I examine how the power of the group over the individual again surfaces, this time in Miller's *Clara.* In this play, we are challenged to consider how adopting a posture of political correctness with respect to a group, particularly a posture that does not penetrate underlying values, causes people to confront the "Other" as representation rather than as individual. Such bigotry can be lethal, even—and perhaps most insidiously—when socially restrained. Categorizing of people, even in politically positive ways, proves deadly in the play, prompting us to consider the full range of damage it can wreak on a culture. In contemporary America, where bigotry commonly comes packaged as racism, classism and homophobia, and where political correctness is practiced even by bigots, Miller is challenging us to define what are *truly* "liberal" values and to consider how extending equality to the group can be practiced without jeopardizing the equality for the individual.

The next two essays in this collection address Miller's depiction of doctors and of marriage, respectively, two roles/institutions historically esteemed, if not in practice then most certainly in the ideal. Stephen Marino's "Physician Heal Thyself" examines Miller's portrayal of doctors and the conflicts between their personal and professional lives. In particular, "Miller's doctors are often misguided; their moral centers are unclear, askew. Their ethics are sometimes questionable. Most importantly, their roles as healers are in direct conflict with their personal desires" (41). Marino examines Miller's doctors across the canon and discovers that "all Miller's doctors confront his great themes of public vs. private guilt and responsibility; however their roles as doctors and healers complicate the tension between these" (42). He concludes, "What every Miller doctor possesses in common is an idealism that clashes with reality. Most often the idealism—whether in their professional or personal lives—thrusts them into a conflict with forces of society which temper their idealism—leaving them forever changed in the process" (42).

Carlos Campo's essay, "Miller, Marriage and Middle America" explores the representation of marriage in Miller's plays. Though the marriages of Miller's characters are flawed, Campo contends, "A close analysis of marriage in Miller's drama seems to suggest not a rejection, but an underlying embrace, however uneasy, of the middle American ideal of marriage" (56). Examining Miller's depiction of marriage in *All My Sons, Death of a Salesman, After the Fall, Broken Glass, The Ride Down Mt. Morgan* and *The Last Yankee*, as well as Miller's own marriage experiences as he relates them in his autobiography *Timebends*, Campo concludes that despite the "sometimes-dark events in his life" and the struggles of his characters with marriage, "it is evident that [Miller] believes that marriage can be a unifying agent in a world of separateness" (56).

The next three essays turn directly to the land itself, exploring how a longing for the pastoral life of rural America asserts itself in Miller's plays. George Castelitto's "Arthur Miller and the Language of Middle America" follows some of Miller's urban-dwelling characters in *A View from the Bridge, Death of a Salesman, The Crucible* and *The Price*, describing how they yearn for "a wider expanse and the possibility of a more socially and psychologically gratifying frontier securely distant from the diminishing and crippling urban construct in which they find themselves" (71). The language of these characters, particularly their "reveries about nature. . .transform the dialogue from urban colloquial to a more mannered, rural rhetoric" (71-72). Juxtaposing confinement and freedom, throughout the characters' speech, "echoes of the American heartland" are detectable, "submerged beneath the urban expressions"—"vowels and syllables that resonate from Middle American roots in both discernibly concrete and metaphorical respects" (Castelitto 72).

William Smith contributes two essays that examine Miller's use of wood imagery, with wood in its natural state (trees, forests) signifying purity and an ancestral link to the early American landscape while wood in an altered state (lumber and structures) represents the corruption of the modern, man-made world. As Smith explains, "For Miller, wood resides at the heart of early American life and represents the instinct to escape the machinations of an increasingly industrial society and return to what one knows best and what one knows **is** best—living in nature and working with one's hands, ultimately generating a transcendental satisfaction not otherwise attainable" (79). In "Figuring Our Past and Present in Wood," Smith examines wood imagery in *The Crucible* and *Death of a Salesman*. Wood and nature are juxtaposed to socially-constructed, unnatural elements—namely the Puritan religion and both the urban enclosures and the definitions of success of city living—to demonstrate "society's threat to individuality" (80).

In "Damn Yankee! Leroy Hamilton Crafts Wood with Passion and Honesty, but Who in Modern America Cares?" Smith describes how Leroy, a carpenter in Miller's *The Last Yankee*, is at odds with the dominant, confining business culture of the world he inhabits, a world represented both by the businessman Frick and by Leroy's materialistic wife, Patricia. Miller likewise contrasts the integrity and values of these characters, suggesting that "honor, tradition and character appear anathema to survival and success in economically driven contemporary America" (Smith 95). Given that the play is set in a mental hospital, Smith also suggests that "the current structure of society, dependent upon business and focused on wealth, leads people inevitably toward an empty, depressed emotional state from which only a connection to the organic can return them" (94).

The final three essays of this volume address reality in various ways, either directly or through memory. In "[S]omewhere down deep where the sources are," Frank Bergmann considers the very real American murder trial of Snyder and Gray in 1927 and its potential impact on Miller's writing of *Death of a Salesman*, though Miller never mentions it as an influence or even having any memory of it. Bergmann suggests that though Miller was just twelve years old at the time, he likely would have been aware of the famous trial, some of the material from which may have founds its way into his writing through subconscious avenues. While individual examples of parallels between facts of the Snyder/Gray trial and details in *Salesman* may be considered coincidental, as a set, they warrant some investigation.

From real world material finding its way into Miller plays, we move to Miller's depiction of reality within his plays. Ashis Sengupta contends that the depiction of reality is more problematic in Miller's later plays than in the earlier ones, where the "real" eventually becomes apparent through layers of "personal delusion and public myth" (Sengupta 107). In the later plays, however, the "real" defies definition and is never fully asserted. This lack of certainty and stability in reality creates an ambiguity for Miller's characters and calls into question "assumptions about an integral self and an integrated society" (108), making the attempt to determine the nature of reality for Miller "a moral issue, finally" (qtd. in Sengupta 108) as the characters seek to assign meaning and value to their experiences.

The problem of defining and accepting the real, particularly as it asserts itself through memory, is explored by Susan Abbotson, who examines the dangers of memory in the 1987 Dramatist Play Service version of Miller's *I Can't Remember Anything*. As Abbotson explains, *I Can't Remember Anything* "deals with that perennial Miller concern, the necessity for people to acknowledge their past as an active part of their current existence" (125). She considers the dangers inherent in neglecting the past—and refusing to learn from it—as well as in overindulging in the past or creating an imagined past.

With this volume, we acknowledge Arthur Miller's contribution to American theatre and American life, knowing that his work remains an active part of our current existence, though the playwright passed away, on February 10, 2005, even as this volume was being edited. He has served as the voice of—and to—America, calling us to examine our collective memory, values, assumptions, and relationships, both to the land and to each other.

Paula T. Langteau
University of Wisconsin Colleges

xii

*The Arthur Miller Society
recognizes the artistry, moral
authority, and human solidarity
of our mentor. We thank
Arthur Miller because
you leave us our name
and social mission.*

(Livesay, *New York Times*, 2/15/05)

Acknowledgments

Tremendous heartfelt thanks to Rhonda Jacobs for her vital assistance with organizing the Eighth International Arthur Miller Conference. I must also recognize Nicolet College, which hosted the event. Special thanks to Leo Hodlofski for his proofreading and Steve Marino for his advice and assistance. His earlier volume, "The Salesman Has a Birthday" paved the way for this one! Finally, I would like to thank the University of Wisconsin Colleges for providing a supportive environment for academic scholarship.

Arthur Miller:
Guardian of the Dream of America

Steven R. Centola

One of the most fascinating images I saw in the newspaper in 2003 appeared in a series of photographic stills published in the February 19, 2003, issue of *The New York Times*. These pictures show what at first glance appears to be an incongruous juxtaposition: a young black rapper named Mos Def is found positioned beside eighty-seven-year-old playwright Arthur Miller. At first glance, one has to wonder what these two artists could possibly have in common. Practitioners of radically different art forms and inheritors of widely differing cultural and racial heritages, they seem to have nothing in common. But it immediately becomes clear that that is simply not the case. The young black rapper and the elderly white playwright on that particular evening had participated in an antiwar protest at a poetry reading at Avery Fisher Hall in New York City. The young black man and the elderly white man joined others—men and women, old and young, black and white; people from various cultural, racial, ethnic, and religious backgrounds who faced the cold winter weather and gathered together for a common cause: to protest the War with Iraq and the cancellation of a poetry reading at the White House prompted by First Lady Laura Bush's fear that anti-war readings there would embarrass her husband at the time of his military incursion into Iraq. This event, and the prominence of Arthur Miller at it, served as a vivid reminder of a simple fact about the role of the literary artist in American society—a role that Arthur Miller has certainly relished and frequently discussed in eloquent and passionate terms throughout his long and distinguished career in the theater.

Not even a week after this anti-war protest in New York City had occurred, Miller was ruminating on this special role for the serious literary artist in American society in an essay published in *The New York Times*, tellingly entitled "Looking for a Conscience." Here, Miller, while musing unhappily about the lack of seriousness of the Broadway theater, and by raising poignant questions about "Broadway's relevance to the life of this world now" ("Conscience" 1), revealed and implicitly defined, with the carefully selected questions he asked, what the role of the literary artist must be, and has always been, in American society. Sounding a little like a weary, fiery Biblical prophet exhorting the masses who have continuously failed to heed his warnings, Miller laments the absence of "acerbic social commentary. . .on the Broadway stage" and challengingly asks whether "a lively, contentious, reflective theater [is] beyond our reach, our imaginations?" ("Conscience" 13). Even more to the heart of the matter, and vividly exemplifying his personal commitment to the role of the writer that he addresses so vigorously in his essay, Miller adeptly links his critique of the Broadway theater to an indictment of officials in the United States government who label critics of the current administration as unpatriotic. It is precisely this all too familiar situation, one involving the use of scare tactics and intimidation to silence detractors of the government, one eerily and ominously reminiscent of those two other dark periods of American history pilloried by Miller in *The Crucible*, that irks the playwright and spurs him to ask: "Has the essence of America, its very nature, changed from benign democracy to imperium?" ("Conscience" 13). With this single question, Miller implicitly addresses the central role—the crucial, inevitable, and pivotal role—for the literary artist in a free society: to serve as the voice of the people who are silenced by fear and intolerance; to ask the challenging and difficult questions of a government, a society, a people that prefers self-congratulatory praise to unflinching moral self-scrutiny; to be the conscience of a nation that finds it uncomfortable to undergo the rigorous examination of the dark recesses of the national psyche and individual soul that earnest and honest self-evaluation necessitate. With his protest against the War in Iraq, and in his continued effort to use literary art to prick the conscience of a nation too easily cowed by the politics of intimidation and a blind obedience to corrupt authority, Miller once again provided firm testimony to his persistent commitment to social justice and human decency and the rights of all people to live with dignity and in peace. This most recent example of the playwright's advocacy for civil liberties and freedom of speech unveils the moral backbone not only of his plays, stories, and essays, but also of his lifetime work to free dissident writers abroad and champion the human rights of the oppressed at home. Art is deeply connected to life, for Arthur Miller; art not only derives from life experience, but it must also respond to life and improve the conditions of life and living for humanity. For this reason, Miller frequently describes all great drama as inherently social in nature. Like Miller, Edward Albee acknowledges the necessity for important art to be socially relevant, and he identifies this shared conviction with Miller as the basis for his celebration of Miller's achievement as a writer. Albee writes: "Arthur Miller understands that serious writing is a social act as well as an aesthetic one, that political involvement comes with the territory. . . . His plays and his conscience are a cold burning force" (qtd. in Bigsby, *Company* 1). Indeed, the intertwined moral and aesthetic imperative that inspired and animated Miller's art resulted in his creation of a body of work that speaks below the surface of the overt drama with a resonance, a highly charged subtext and equally rich cultural context, about the possibility and failure of America—America as a concept, an ideal, a cluster of myths and cultural stereotypes, a nation, a government and governance system, a people, a character, and an impossible, forever elusive, but always inspiring, dream. Miller's critique and celebration of America underlies and informs every facet of his plays and places this great playwright in a long procession of significant American writers who have responded similarly to the challenge and the glory of this dream called America.

Driven by a belief in the conception of providential history, the earliest record-keepers of the search for a new order in the New World, the Puritans, left a legacy that would strongly affect perspectives of America for hundreds of years. These cultural custodians of the dream of America strove to create a perfect moral order in the wilderness that confronted them. Undaunted by its contradictions and complexities, they steadfastly pursued their dream of America as a New Eden, a New Jerusalem, a City upon a Hill that promised the possibility of moral perfection and personal redemption. Undeterred from promulgating their own propaganda about the dream of America, these early wayfarers who chronicled and grappled with their own dark voyages into the private corners of the human soul forged for posterity a vision of the dream of America that would tantalize, beguile, frustrate, and inspire writers for many years to come. In their own day, the Puritans vacillated between hope and despair, as their dream of spiritual salvation met opposition from the reality of indigenous people whose foreign customs and unfamiliar religious practices located them appropriately, and irrevocably, in the mental landscape of the Puritans, with the frightening, and all-inspiring, wilderness in which the native inhabitants resided. Wrestling with their own consciences and warring with their strange new neighbors, these self-declared custodians of the golden dream found themselves inveigled in violent power struggles antithetical to their orthodox Christian principles. Ultimately, they handed down to succeeding generations a legacy built on contradictions, a fiercely held conviction that redemption was possible, that happiness could be attained in the New World through hard work and individual human enterprise, that the self could be perfected, that the sacred and the secular could be wed in the promise, the hope, the dream that was America—and all of this was possible, they believed, despite the fact that many indigenous people were slaughtered and un-Christian violence permeated the way of life in this new frontier.

By the 19th Century, following the tumultuous birth and expansion of a nation and the development of laws and regulations that would guide the masses searching for a free and democratic existence in an oftentimes inhospitable environment, practitioners of an ignoble self-reliance and rugged individualism became the robber barons whose avarice and cupidity tarnished the agrarian dream and turned it into a urban nightmare. Disillusioned by slavery, the incessant forced relocation of indigenous peoples following a series of broken treaties, the progressive devastation of the natural landscape as the transcontinental railroad brought with it endless development, and the systematic dismantling of the Jeffersonian ideal with the steady movement toward the incorporation of America, writers such as Emerson, Thoreau, Melville, Whitman, Twain, Crane, Dreiser, and others found themselves inevitably gravitating toward their role as guardians of the dream. Delivering scathing indictments against those corrosive forces in business, industry, the military, and the government obsessed with the accumulation of wealth and power, these writers shared a fervent desire to investigate honestly their own lives as well as the problems of their society. They possessed inordinate courage and tremendous moral strength as they created a body of literature that held a mirror up to themselves and their society and looked unblinkingly at the uncovered social deformities and personal failings that resided there. By debunking dominant myths, and by aggressively and honestly addressing real challenges to national ideals, these guardians of the dream of America simultaneously provided a means for taking corrective action that would lead to a better and improved society and a path to moral self-improvement for the denizens of the young nation.

In succeeding generations, deep into the 20th Century and even now at the start of the 21st Century, various intellectuals—literary writers and cultural historians alike—would wrestle with their own confusion about what it meant to be an American, what burden and obligation, what privileges and benefits, what traditions and inheritances, what myths and contradictions awaited them in their own personal exploration of the society and culture that surrounded and enveloped them. Writers such as Fitzgerald, Ellison, Wright, Morrison, Ginsberg, Pynchon, Williams, Albee, Shepard and others would also weigh in with their own brand of social criticism, exposing the hidden lies and underlying illusions fostered in a society built upon public myths and nationalistic pride. Examining various challenges to the sense of personal identity inherent in a pluralistic society and exploring questions related to the possibility for an authentic existence in a chaotic, disordered, and fragmented society, these writers gave voice to the marginalized and alienated and infused a spirit of protest in writings which continued to advocate and uphold the principles of human decency in human affairs even in the midst of cultural and historical entropy.

Like these other guardians of the dream of America, Arthur Miller simultaneously preserves the dream of America even while attacking and revealing the gross deficiencies of the materialistic values and cultural myths that have traditionally defined and limited American society's understanding of the American dream. For like Emerson, Twain, Fitzgerald, and other great writers in the American procession, Miller recognizes that the dream of America is more than just an American dream. The American ethos that served as the ideological foundation for a nation essentially existed more as an idea than as an actuality. It essentially had little to do with affluence and the consumer culture, but rather represented the possibility for hope and the opportunity to live freely. Miller articulates this notion well when he writes: "the values this country has stood for in the past . . . have helped to keep alive a promise of a democratic future for the world" (*Theater Essays* 87-88). The promise of such a future is one

for the entire world, and not just for American society. The hope that
is America, its promise of a better life, its inherent sense of
possibility, is a universal dream that transcends culture, ideology, and
geography, and that speaks to all people of all societies and all ages.
As Miller told me in an interview in August 2001, the dream is a
"more-than-American dream." Therefore, in articulating this global
view of the dream of America, Miller establishes an important
correlation between the treatment of American society in his drama
and the development of thematic material that transcends the local
and particular subject matter in his plays and speaks universally about
issues affecting all of humanity. This is certainly nothing new and is
consistent with the achievement of all great writers: the universal can
only be achieved through the particular. However, this explanation
helps to clarify the fundamental significance of Miller's role as a
social dramatist because it shows how he can ultimately examine the
whole of society—and the world—through his focus on a particular
family's, or a single individual's, conflict in his drama.

Of all the powerful drama Miller has created, it is *Death of a
Salesman* (1949) that most completely illustrates Miller's remarkable
ability to comment on a timelessly and universally significant issue
through his isolation and concentration on the crisis that occurs in a
particular family in American society, and most notably the patriarch
in that family—and unquestionably this extraordinary achievement at
least partially accounts for this play's greatness. Critical discussions
of this play over the years have centered mostly on Miller's handling
of the "success myth." As Brenda Murphy and Susan Abbotson have
pointed out, "While there has been some effort to defend Miller as an
upholder of the American Dream, most critics who have written on
this subject have attempted to explain Willy's demise as a failure on
his, and often Miller's part, to comprehend American history and
values" (*Understanding* 5). Undeniably, Willy does indeed fail to
understand the intricacy of the workings of American history and the
complexity and oftentimes inherently contradictory aspects of
American values. But the same cannot be said of Miller. Over a span
of almost sixty years, this great playwright has repeatedly
demonstrated his incredible skill at interpreting and understanding
American historical experience in his prose nonfiction writings.
From the start of his career until the present, Miller has used the essay
form as a way of providing insightful commentary on the urgencies of
social change affecting, and sometimes transforming, not just
American society, but also the world. In several books of reportage,

in his autobiography, *Timebends* (1987), in his collected *Theater Essays* (1996), and in the more overtly political pieces assembled in *Echoes Down the Corridor* (2000), Miller comments insightfully on the vagaries of historical event and shows a particularly sound grasp of the incidents in American history that affected his writing of such plays as *Death of a Salesman*, *The Crucible* (1953), *The American Clock* (1980), and *Broken Glass* (1994). Throughout his career, Miller definitely has proven over and over again that he does indeed understand American history and values. In one memorable essay after another, he captures the frenzied spirit of a schizophrenic society and records poignant observations on the political unrest and moral decline ravaging his country.

In such plays as *Death of a Salesman* and *The Crucible*, as well as in his memoirs and essays, Miller's historical vision is enlarged by his remarkable ability to synthesize past and present circumstance and to find in the immediate event a corresponding analogue whose example is instructive and perhaps even curative to a national psyche fractured by its own internal contradictions. In *Death of a Salesman*, in particular, Miller succeeds in showing that everything is interrelated, and time is but a flimsy veil that sometimes masks the underlying connective tissue that binds all of human experience together. But it is not just the past and the present, or the world and America, that are united in *Death of a Salesman* and the rest of Miller's work. Miller also interweaves his criticism of American cultural myths with his individual reading of the workings and failures of history. The end result, says Robert A. Martin, is that "the twin concepts of truth and morality" loom large "as the highest priority in his work" (*Theater Essays* xxi). These principles motivate everything Miller writes and also underlie his life work for human rights and the protection of people's civil liberties. Chris Bigsby identifies this "moral imperative" as the matrix behind Miller's aesthetics and artistic vision. Bigsby writes: "For Miller, beyond the fantasies, the self-deceptions, the distortions of private and public myths are certain obligations which cannot be denied. The present cannot be severed from the past or the individual from his social context; that, after all, is the basis of his dramatic method and of his moral faith" (*Modern American Drama* 124). When an individual like Willy Loman violates this basic law of human nature, he unintentionally sets into motion a chain of circumstances that cannot be controlled and that inevitably will force a reckoning. "The structure of a play is always the story of how birds came home to roost," Miller is fond of saying in interviews and essays, and in his portrayal of Willy's demise in *Death of a Salesman*, as the "hidden" is "unveiled" and "the inner laws of reality. . .announce themselves . . ." (*Theater Essays* 179), text, subtext, and cultural context come together in a brilliantly organic fusion to produce a modern-day masterpiece.

Underlying and embedded throughout the text is a rich and dense subtext that raises unresolved questions and endless speculation about the characters, their relationships, their motivation and behavior, their dreams and failures, their incongruous speech and action, and the problematic nature of the society that witnesses their collapse. Undeniably, on one level, the subtext calls into question the whole system of capitalist enterprise in a material society that equates individual worth with success. The opening stage directions, for example, resonate with powerful symbolic suggestiveness and speak to the overwhelming force of society crashing down on the individual. Thomas Adler effectively describes how this scenery and the play's setting embed "theatrical and social meaning in the play" (Roudané 24). Adler also comments on the way music provides an "ironic counterpoint" to the stage image. This important device is instrumental in calling to the audience's mind important subtextual meaning linking Willy's dream of success to Jeffersonian idealism and the 19th Century romantic belief in "freedom and expansiveness and possibility" (Roudané 47). Through Miller's effective orchestration of lighting, music, movement, speech, and action, the stage—and the stage apron in particular—become the mind of Willy Loman, and as Miller unravels this complex and disorderly mind before us, we see not only the unresolvable tensions and contradictory values that are in perpetual conflict inside Willy Loman, but also find echoes and remnants of the paradoxical, and oftentimes clashing ideological, political, economic, and social concepts and principles upon which the nation, its cultural myths, and its values have been constructed, tested, adjusted, altered, and transformed. The use of expressionistic dislocations, especially, in the temporal and spatial progression in the play also shows the effect of social pressure on individual psychology—an issue not overtly discussed but clearly a central thematic concern in this play and most of Miller's drama. This theme has been discussed repeatedly as the central point of intersection in Miller's plays between private tensions and public issues, which in *Death of a Salesman* is evident everywhere—from the characterization, action, form, language, scenery, and dramatic strategy to its beautifully crafted and highly innovative style of representation. In Chris Bigsby's view, this remarkable fusion of form and theme in *Death of a Salesman* not only captures "the structure of experience and thought," but also shows "how private and public history cohere" (*Modern American Drama* 85). For as Bigsby reminds us, in Salesman *in Beijing*, Miller describes *Death of a Salesman* to his Chinese cast as "a love story between a man and his son, and in a crazy way between both of them and America" (qtd. in *Modern American Drama* 86), and Bigsby rightly adds that what "is true of the play. . .[is] true, too, of Miller, for whom America has proven a wayward mistress worthy of redemption" (*Modern American Drama* 86). Bigsby explains the correlation between this central thematic issue in the play and Miller's own personal love/hate affair with American society in the following statement:

> Believing, as he does, that the artist is by nature a dissident, committed to the necessity of challenging the given, he is equally compelled by a country which, despite its conservatism, is paradoxically committed to transformation. An immigrant society, what else could it propose? Its animating myths all cohere around the proposition that change is a central imperative. The true American is protean. The problem is that the imagination—the seat of personal and social change—is too easily usurped by the facile fantasy, that urbanization and the brittle satisfactions of the material world breed spiritual inertia and a failure of will. It is for this reason that Miller finds in his most self-deceiving and marginalized characters a dignity that derives from their refusal to settle for simple accommodation. (*Modern American Drama* 86)

In this respect, then, it becomes clear why discussion of any play by Arthur Miller, and particularly of *Death of a Salesman*, requires careful consideration of the cultural context underlying the play's composition, construction, productions, and reception. As Matthew Roudané and others have convincingly argued, *Death of a Salesman* may be, despite its many universal themes and strong international appeal, "the quintessential American drama" (Roudané 23), for "the play captures something truthful about contemporary American experience—particularly in its display of American linguistic cadence, focus on the family (dis)unity, versions of the American dream myth, [perspective on] the relation between business and one's

self-validation, [and] questions of representation and gender"
(Roudané 23).

The main challenge for audiences today, particularly the younger
readers and members of the audience experiencing Miller's drama for
the first time, might be the absence of a frame of reference for
understanding even the most basic historical references in the play.
For example, audiences not familiar with the era of the Great
Depression might fail to immediately grasp the significance of
Willy's constant references to 1928 as the year of his greatest
professional success. Some historical perspective would undoubtedly
demonstrate how devastating were the consequences of the economic
crisis that threatened to topple the entire society during this time
period. In fact, new audiences might greatly benefit from knowing
that, in his essays and interviews, Miller repeatedly points out how
the Great Depression shaped his artistic vision and permanently
affected his understanding of the intersection between public and
private acts of betrayal and cruelty. The social crisis had a powerful
impact on the family and no one in American society at that time
could escape that predicament. 1928, therefore, the year before the
stock market crash, has special meaning inside Willy's unreliable
memory because it serves for him as a vivid reminder of a time when
he still enjoyed the love and respect of his family and did not have to
deal with the intense financial hardship he all but certainly faced,
along with the rest of American society, during the Great Depression.

Equally significant in this drama is the periodic allusion to a time
when greater harmony existed in society, the family, and the
workplace. This idyllic past is associated with an agrarian world
view, one resplendent with open vistas and endless possibilities, and
this highly romantic, perhaps even naively idealistic, view of an
America removed from the competition, commercialization, and
dehumanization associated with the present action in the play stands
in stark contrast to both Miller's formative experiences during the
Great Depression and the post World-War II time period in which the
play is written and produced. The conflation of these conflicting
representations of America—the place, the society, its values as well
as its promises and failings—imbues the play with tremendous
ambiguity, which Roudané says creates the play's "multivalent
textures" that foster "multivocal cultural attitudes" from teachers and
students alike who, in open and energetic class discussions, can test
the "cultural essentialism" implicit in a traditional reading of the play
(Roudané 23).

Likewise, the hegemony inherent both in the Loman family and the society upon which the characters are based is also a subject that warrants critical examination and intense deconstruction. The patriarchal order so prevalent at any age of the American historical progression even finds itself almost directly deposed in the unorthodox and highly innovative interpretations of the character of Linda Loman by actresses such as Elizabeth Franz in her 1999 Broadway performance and Zhu Lin in the 1983 Beijing production of the play. The cultural myth that relegates men to a position of dominance and women to a role of relative submission in the family in American society is indisputably called into question by the remarkable performances of these two actresses. Hence, in this intriguing fusion of performance issues and cultural critique in Miller's drama, we happily discover a powerful contextual linkage for audiences in today's society that seek some means of finding their own personal connection to the play and its characters.

Maybe even more significant, ultimately, is the attention Miller's play gives to questions pertaining to work alienation and the concomitant identity crisis it fosters for those in American society like Willy Loman, who are trained to believe that their self-worth rests entirely on their profit margin or net worth. Indoctrinated with the success-formula platitudes and get-rich-quick schemes popularized by Dale Carnegie, Russell Conwell, and others in the early twentieth century, Willy Loman becomes the ultimate embodiment of the outer-directed organization man who sacrifices personal integrity and any shred of human dignity in his relentless quest to achieve the forever-elusive American dream of material success. By embracing the fraudulent values of his venal society in his fanatical pursuit of his impossible dream, Willy relinquishes control over his life and unwittingly sets in motion the chain of circumstances that eventually bring about his demise.

So how can audiences today appreciate and understand the complex vision of a playwright who simultaneously memorializes and subverts the animating cultural myths of our society? Can the audience who lacks direct experience with the historical context or the cultural heritage that is part of the intellectual framework underpinning Miller's play access its codes of meaning and derive from the reading or stage experience a full and deep appreciation of the dilemma confronting the Loman family? I definitely believe the answer is yes, if they discover for themselves the relevance of Miller's exploration of these cultural issues, in particular, to their own personal lives. Just as the Chinese audiences in Beijing in 1983 discovered the Lomans in themselves, when they reacted enthusiastically to Miller's unfamiliar western drama with thunderous ovations, so too can audiences today recognize their own likeness in the disturbing stage images depicting the collapse of the Lomans and the menacing detachment of the impersonal society threatening to destroy them. Like the Lomans, audiences in American society today have inevitably struggled uneasily within the love/hate battleground of family relations, have questioned whether their identity is restricted exclusively to the kind of personal achievement oftentimes associated with job performance reviews or academic success, and have adopted the cultural expectation that the success myth is supposed to drive their educational opportunities, work experience, and even regulate a good part of their marital life. Like Willy, some members of the audience in American society today almost certainly know from direct personal experience what it means to feel displaced from their chosen image of themselves, and these alienated and dispossessed dreamers of the golden dream understand the difficulty, and maybe even the futility, of standing up to a system that denies them the right to express their unique personalities. Maybe the unfortunate circumstances of their lives makes them predisposed to understand how Willy, like Ralph Ellison's *Invisible Man*, actually speaks for them, and for all the disenfranchised and socially displaced, on some lower frequency than they are ordinarily accustomed to hearing. And in this respect so too does the play, particularly in its expose and implicit critique of the cultural myths that limit choices and constantly threaten to divide and dehumanize society.

Death of a Salesman, like all of Arthur Miller's drama, offers its audiences a searing indictment not only of those who substitute lies for reality and illusions for truth, but also of the society that manufactures and markets those lies and illusions to a nation of dreamers and devotees of the ever receding future where hope for success and personal salvation lie. Yet even though this play, as well as the rest of Miller's drama, critically addresses the moral bankruptcy concealed beneath the façade of American material success, there simultaneously exists an opposing tendency in Miller's work to romanticize the mythology of the American West and the agrarian ideal deeply embedded in American thought and permanently shaping and transforming American values. This twin vision of America as both sordid reality and sublime possibility permeates the playwright's work. In this respect, Miller's comments about Mark Twain could also aptly be used to describe his own ambivalent position toward his country: "He seems to have seen his role, and probably the role of literature in general, differently than most cultural observers presently see theirs. He is not using his alienation from the public illusions of his hour in order to reject his country implicitly as though he could live without it, but manifestly in order to correct it. . . .[H]e is very much part of what needs changing" (*Echoes* 256).

Miller has always recognized and accepted the need for the artist to oppose and confound the sources of cruel and impersonal power that threaten to destroy democracy in American society, and he did so even at his own personal risk and at the possibility of placing his career and reputation in jeopardy. His risked imprisonment and alienation from his society when he courageously defied the directive from the House Un-American Activities Committee to turn informant against others, and he repeatedly placed his own liberty and life in danger by working tirelessly to free dissident writers from imprisonment in foreign countries that act without respect for the basic freedoms that the playwright so highly prizes and associates with the best that is America. His politics almost certainly cost him the Nobel Prize early in his career and undeniably had a negative impact on the critical reception his plays have received at various times in this country. Yet, despite the undeniable injury his career would sustain as a result of his political activism and personal crusades, Miller never swerved from his heartfelt conviction that to maintain his honor, he had to acknowledge his personal responsibility for others and choose never to "commit [himself] to anything [he] did not consider somehow useful in living one's life" (*Timebends* 547). In his art, this form of social commitment resulted in his deciding that "writing had to try to save America. . ." (*Timebends* 547).

This custodian of the dream that is America—a dream that Miller quotes Archibald MacLeish as saying "was promises" (*Timebends* 114)—possesses the "moral strenuousness and strength," as Malcolm Bradbury puts it, that were necessary to create a "theatre of self-questioning democratic dissent" (qtd. in *Company* 186). With his "habitual dedication to justice, mercy, dignity, and truth," writes Joseph Heller, Miller puts "his integrity and uncontrived ethical sensibility into his plays," and thereby creates stage art "that is unsurpassed in our lifetime" (qtd. in *Company* 3). For this reason, Arthur Miller stands tall in the procession of great American writers who have wrestled with the shifting and oftentimes contradictory meaning and reality of the American experience. In a letter to the playwright in honor of his seventy-fifth birthday, another important writer of the last century, Ralph Ellison, writes one of the most eloquent and astute commentaries about Miller's artistic achievement. Ellison writes: "Through your art you affirm the democratic vision by redeeming and making visible the marvelous diversity of the human condition. And by giving voice to the voiceless you provide perception to all those who have the heart and courage to see. In other words, you've been an eloquent explorer of America's turbulent and ever-shifting social hierarchy, and by reducing its chaos to artistic form you've given us a crucial gift of national self-consciousness" (qtd. in *Company* 1). This writer who has been characterized as the conscience of a nation, of a historical time period, even of the entire human race has repeatedly given audiences of his drama a vision of hope and possibility that is the true legacy of the dream, the promise, the idea that is America. That extraordinary achievement is, indeed, the lasting legacy of Arthur Miller: guardian of the dream.

Works Cited

Bigsby, Christopher. *Arthur Miller and Company*. London: Methuen, 1990.

————. *Modern American Drama 1945-1990*. Cambridge: Cambridge University Press, 1992.

Martin, Robert A. and Steven R. Centola, eds. *The Theater Essays of Arthur Miller*. New York: Da Capo, 1996.

Miller, Arthur. *Echoes Down the Corridor*. Edited by Steven R. Centola. New York: Viking Penguin, 2000.

————. "Looking for a Conscience." *The New York Times* February 23, 2003, Section 2: 1, 13.

————. *Timbends: A Life*. New York: Grove, 1987.

Murphy, Brenda and Susan C. W. Abbotson, eds. *Understanding* Death of a Salesman. Westport, CT: Greenwood, 1999.

Roudané, Matthew. *Approaches to Teaching Miller's* Death of a Salesman. New York: The Modern Language Association of America, 1995.

Hegemony, Hatred, and the Scapegoat Mechanism in two Miller Dramas — *Playing for Time* and *The Crucible*

Lewis Livesay

Much in American history, such as the Indian genocide and early religious intolerance, conveniently gets erased in the interest of creating a national mythology that celebrates ideals of diversity and freedom. We live in a world that Zygmunt Bauman recently described as a "radical melting" of truths, origins, and interior restraints, resulting in a new order in which "free agents. . .remain radically disengaged, to by-pass each other instead of meeting" (5). When the truth gets lost or too easily glossed over, for whatever reason, a writer like Arthur Miller will accept the responsibility to make us remember that beginnings are never quite as pure as myth implies them to be. We must forever face and reinterpret the struggles and conflicts from which we issue, because as Miller understands, in the words of George Santayana, "Those who cannot remember the past are condemned to repeat it" (284). Miller wrote *The Crucible* to ensure that we will not readily forget how the paranoiac pursuit of anti-American sentiment during the McCarthy years *repeats* the intolerance rampant in early Salem intolerance and persecution. Any community, seeking to purify itself by annihilating every taint of otherness, promotes a totalitarian vision. Good people must realize that utopias run the risk of becoming fascist organizations when ideals of togetherness are upheld through exclusion. Miller points out, in the stage notes to *The Crucible*, the unfortunate human tendency in which "all organization is and must be grounded on the idea of exclusion and prohibition" (6). *The Crucible* and *Playing for Time* present us with Miller's two great dramatizations of organizations fueled by intolerance. And amazingly enough, amidst these dramas of inhumane brutality, Arthur Miller will reveal to us images of human courage and altruism that offer cause for hope.

Many demons drove Joseph McCarthy to see himself as an absolute protector of American values, thus justifying in his mind an assault on values and people who threatened his ideal of America. We hear in *The Crucible* one fleeting echo of McCarthy's famous question "Are you now or have you ever been a member of the Communist Party?"; this moment comes, weighted with irony, in Act Three, when Danforth asks Proctor: "*Have you ever* seen the Devil?" (84)—the ironic twist being that it is the interrogator who has in effect become demonic in his accusatory zeal to exclude another. In a fascist organization, the judge assumes dual right to accuse and convict. Faced with this situation, Proctor cannot point out the obvious as any rebuttal of the holier-than-thou judge would only inflame the community's rapidly rising paranoia and its concomitant need for a sacrificial scapegoat. This scene may very well remind us of how Jesus avoids eye contact with the mob while trying to deflect anger from Mary Magdalene when she is about to be stoned. As René Girard explains, Jesus realizes that he must avoid eye contact, which would provoke a "mimetic contagion" (*Satan* 26); thus, Jesus averts his glance, keeping his focus upon figures that he is sketching in the dirt with his finger (*Satan* 59). In Girard's reading, Jesus does not want to engage the mob from fear that they might decide to substitute him as the victim to alleviate their wrath. Anger always seeks a target. This awareness explains Proctor's trepidation before the bench. In Miller's play, as in life, paranoia is sustained by a will to accusation. Paul Ricoeur, in "The Demythization of Accusation," has noted how Kantian law and Freudian father are held in place as ideals by "the false transcendence of the imperative" accusation that creates a myth of unity (336). Someone must be excluded for the totalitarian state to solidify itself. This sacrificial condition makes us realize why, in a hierarchical social order with an imbalance of power, citizens need protection from those who possess privilege. Whatever is good about our American society issues from a belief in diversity and how no one person should be allowed the power to control the destiny of another as both judge and jury.

The Crucible and *Playing for Time* present visions of idealism gone wrong in which masters exercise a right to accuse and punish others for being different and contaminating their social order. In a world where might makes right, the weak will forever be victimized by the strong. Only with a regulating order, a third term, can we ensure that the self–other binary does not transpose into a Master–Slave relation. This third term, of course, depends on how we write and maintain law. This law must be kept within the realm of social debate, and never be assimilated to the more totalitarian impulses of religious or fanatical dictates. In fact, just recently, Miller has proclaimed that the Salem witch-hunt may be seen as having inspired "the wall of separation between church and state in America, for in Salem theocratic government had its last hurrah" ("Clinton" 269). Despite conservative attacks claiming otherwise, Miller has always been a strong exponent of law and order; he is a pragmatist who believes in regulation, and nothing, I would venture to say, appears to need more vigilant regulation than the foundation of our society based in the theory of the two swords, keeping church and state forever separate.

Playing for Time and *The Crucible* feature totalitarian attempts to impose a purified homogeneity upon society. Blood sacrifice is demanded in any "rites of spring" to unify a paranoid community. The Nazis could not be the Nazis without the Jews, and the Puritans could not be the Puritans without their witches. These two plays dramatize social extremes demanding that all members of a group be the same. Any "otherness" or difference must be identified and obliterated. Freud opens *Group Psychology and the Analysis of the Ego* with the observation that "in the individual's mental life someone else is invariably involved, as a model, as an object, as a helper, as an opponent" (69). This observation depends of course on that mechanism called "the Oedipal complex." Each human starts life connected to a mother, and for most of us, that first connection to a primary caretaker is symbiotic. It is pre-relational. The child exists assimilated to the body of another who provides all that the infant needs to remain in a utopian bliss. Slowly, the child becomes aware of being usurped. If the first human emotion is a pre-relational sense of maternal love, the second emotion, prompted by the father, is relational hate. Love begins as a passive emotion, one to which the human tragically may feel entitled, and then hate can be understood as the first active emotion. Oedipal longing, as Freud describes it, leads the child to want to possess the mother and kill the father to sustain the original state prior to the order of individuality and relations. This longing for utopian bliss presupposes excluding the third, namely paternal authority. As we all know, Freud goes on to explain that maturation demands the child must separate from the mother, seeking a substitute as love object, while the child must simultaneously learn to identify with the power and authority of the father. Oedipalization requires giving up the mother as direct love object and stifling initial rage and hatred aimed at the father. This development comes at a price: we never entirely relinquish our quest to sustain symbiosis; desire for a love that is pre-relational gets repressed into the unconscious, where it continues to foment. The tragedy of life is that no relation to another, no matter how intense or fulfilling, can ever parallel the completeness and abundance of symbiotic absorption into what Jacques Lacan calls "the libidinous investment on the mother's body—a mythical stage, certainly" (256). At the same time, the hatred first targeted at the father also has to be repressed or the individual will never learn to adjust to social authority. Respect for law imposes limits that dictate how human energy must be channeled through acceptable restraints. In *Group Psychology* and *Civilization and its Discontents,* Freud projects the Oedipal complex onto society. In fascism, we discern the attempt to return to a maternal-like absorption through immersion in a group feverishly united to share a common dream. Freud warns that "in a group the individual is brought under conditions which allow him to throw off the repressions of his unconscious instinctual impulses" (*Group* 74). A lessening of restraint activates primordial aggression that must be assuaged by sacrifice. In fascism, *like* bonds with *like*, as the group then seeks to target for sacrifice any interloper marked with threatening difference. According to Freud in *Totem and Taboo*, we must confront this very disconcerting possibility that social organization is founded in satisfying a repressed need through institutionalized murder:

> The violent primal father had doubtless been the feared and envied model of each one of the company of brothers: and in the act of [killing and] devouring him they accomplished their identification with him, and each one of them acquired a portion of his strength. The totem meal, which is perhaps mankind's earliest festival, would thus be a repetition and a commemoration of this memorable and criminal deed, which was the beginning of so many things—of social organization, of moral restrictions and of religion. (142)

Not just social order, but religion, originates in violence—a point attested to by René Girard in his *Violence and the Sacred*. This position makes sense when we allow for how violence so often energizes zealotry. Freud's discovery of a destructive mechanism at the core of exclusionary organizations helps us to understand the fanaticism that Miller is exploring in *Playing for Time* and *The Crucible*.

Miller's plays—from *The Crucible* to his most recent work, *Resurrection Blues*—focus very much on failed societies. In these dramas we can read how ego, with its formation out of the first active emotion, namely hatred, disrupts social relationship. The inherently violent need to find a scapegoat and kill someone in order to sustain a society is a social sickness that potentially pervades organization. *Group Psychology* presents a theory of identification motivated by blood-lust. The protagonist in *Playing for Time* makes a telling remark about such sickness toward the end of the play. At this point Fania Fénelon has spent years in a concentration camp, frequently fawning before her Nazi torturers and negotiating space and food with fellow inmates. With the Allied forces approaching the camp, Fania becomes convinced that she and her fellow prisoners will never be freed because the Nazis will have to kill them to eliminate witnesses to years of atrocities. This thought of death provides relief because Fania suspects that she would never be able to return to normalcy, having seen what she has seen. Fania declares, "All I mean is that we may be innocent, but we have changed. I mean we know a little something about the human race that we didn't know before. And it's not good news" (78). Having been a targeted victim, a scapegoat, for Nazi hatred of difference, Fania has looked into how extreme organization unleashes an aggression to destroy. This sadistic urge to destroy otherness and create a social order without any taint of difference disgusts Fania. This character's ethical response to the barbarity of extreme hegemony aimed at excluding otherness conveys Miller's attitude toward intolerance. *The Crucible* and *Playing for Time* both reveal how repressed aggression can reemerge as hegemonic totalitarianism sanctioning murder. The history of the world, to this day, is a record of one attempted genocide after another. At our conference site, in Wisconsin, a state that does better than most with allocating land for native-American reservations, we should never forget that this country was founded upon a genocide.

Readers who know Miller mainly through *Death of a Salesman* could very easily conclude that Miller's version of tragedy issues from problems tied to the individual's ego. A psychoanalytic interpretation of this play can argue that Willy's inability to enter into the symbolic order of differences keeps him from crossing the oedipal threshold into a world of social relations. Instead of accepting a world of substitutes, exchanges, and differentials, Willy remains transfixed within the fantasy life of his own ego, putting himself at the center of his universe. All humans do this from time to time in daydreams, but Willy's fantasy-life dominates his interpersonal connections. This leads Biff at the end of the play to assert the social order when he dethrones the ego by declaring: "Pop! I'm a dime a dozen, and so are you!" (132). Willy, of course, rejects that view. Willy's refusal to acknowledge the social order of how money, status, identity, and social relations are all commodities to be exchanged and negotiated delimits his ability to enter the social realm: "I am not a dime a dozen! I am Willy Loman, . . ." (132). Lured by that elusive and seductive American dream, which promises self-centered fulfillment reenacting abundant maternal bliss, Willy escapes life through a wish-fulfillment dreaming about his kingly ascendancy. He is cut off from the differential exchange, which prevails in the social order, preferring to live in a private world that emanates from his ego. The commonplace salesman sells himself the ultimate con job: he does not have to grow up and compete in a social realm that is pretty tough, cutthroat, and frequently unforgiving. Willy is literally a long way from ever seeing himself as the mythic Dave Singleman, the salesman known and adored in death—in his absence from life. In a parallel absence effected through fantasy, Willy figuratively becomes Dave. Willy's own identification with Dave leads him to take his leave from life as absent father, firmly convinced that his "death wish" will fulfill his ego's dream of initiating his son, Biff, as princely heir to Willy's kingly throne: "Can you imagine that magnificence with twenty thousand dollars in his pocket?" (135). Willy buys into the ego's dream of self-fulfillment making him feel supreme beyond any sober and literal appraisal of his net-worth in a world where he lacks the power and status that his unrestrained ego ravenously craves. Willy's dream, as Charley reminds us at the end, is everyone's dream: "A salesman is got to dream, boy. It comes with the territory" (138). The longing to dream is thoroughly human and American; it explains what makes Willy part of each one of us. It is the secret to his universal appeal, but that secret provides a pathway to our insight into the death wish. By clinging to the dream and turning one's back on the social order, an individual, in this case Willy, embraces "the death wish" of Thanatos. We sometimes refuse to want to live, and instead we long to die because social life and its order of relations simply do not provide the totality that unrestrained ego demands. No relation can ever emulate maternal symbiosis.

In the social realm, we can see the lure of totalitarian thought. Totalitarianism is nothing other than the ego writ large on a grandiose scale. In both *Playing for Time* and *The Crucible*, Arthur Miller creates dramatic parallels to what Freud accomplished in projecting the destructive impulse within individual ego onto the social landscape. In *Civilization and its Discontents*, Freud examines how insecurity and rivalry destabilize social organization. In coming to terms with Freud or Miller, we must confront evil. It is right there at the origin of conscious life in the first actively human emotion, the hatred that the infant feels to the invading third that breaks up its pre-conscious, pre-relational, sustained symbiosis within the mother/child union. Miller's plays powerfully contain an awareness that the taint of evil intrinsically pervades each one inside our social organization. Evil is not just Hitler or Puritanical judges or McCarthy; evil is human. It is endemic to the process of trying to live together. It can be restrained, but never eliminated. It can rear its ugly head in Salem, in Wisconsin, in Washington, in Europe—anywhere and everywhere.

In *Playing for Time*, Miller is dramatizing the real-life concentration camp experiences of Fania Fénelon, a half-Jewish cabaret singer, whose ordeals at Auschwitz and Bergen-Belsen are recounted in her autobiography, entitled *Playing for Time*. Miller first adapted this work as a screenplay for a cable television film, starring Vanessa Redgrave and Jane Alexander, both of whom won Emmies for their work. Miller later set this story for the stage, and that is the text to which I refer. This play, surprisingly, has never received a major production; recently, Martin Gottfried described this drama as "Miller's most emotional play since *Death of a Salesman*" and lamented that its potential as theatre still "remains to be discovered" (417). At the beginning of the play, the character of Fania Fénelon makes clear that she wants to survive her incarceration by never participating in the petty rivalries that motivate many of the women in the camp. Helpless to oppose the real oppressor, many of the women play mind-games with each other in order to establish some remnant of status at another's expense. Hence, the hierarchy established by Naziism is ironically mirrored within the camp, suggesting the universality of evil. Fania understands how this avarice to be one-up on another in status and food will consume any last vestige of redeeming dignity. One of the secrets for survival that carries Fania along is her capacity to annul her ego. Fania refuses to allow herself to be reduced to a self-absorbed creature. Early in the play Fania says to one of the Polish Blockawas, "I have to say one thing to you, dear. You alarm me. Because it's not that you haven't enough. It's that whatever anybody else has, you have to have more. And if that catches on here, we are finished!" (29). Discerning quite realistically that the food supply in a concentration camp is severely limited and that the demand among prisoners is highly competitive to the point that if they share none of them will make it, Etalina responds, "But, Fania, we can't very well share everything." To which Fania can only reply, "I refuse to turn into an animal for a gram of margarine or a potato peel!" (29). Miller's characterization of Fania suggests how we always have a choice to make in approaching the *other*. For Fania, her significant interactions are with fellow prisoners. Jay Halio reads Fania as a courageous character who refuses to fall "into despair" (130). Fania resists the human tendency to scapegoat another. By contrast, failed oedipalization can be read in the character of Marianne who responds to Fania as a mentor with whom Marianne is having an alternating love/hate relationship. Kimberly Cook notes this pattern: "Marianne becomes increasingly more dependent upon and, ironically, more resentful of Fania" (100). From this we can conclude that oedipalization contains the ultimate source of irony, in the sense that Freud and the best artists have revealed to us how life contains the seeds of its own undoing. The type of jealousy and incipient rivalry evident in Marianne reveals how Thanatos is at least as deeply entrenched in the human psyche as Eros. Asserting the redemptive viewpoint, Susan C.W. Abbotson concludes her reading of this play by reminding us: "If everyone shares a capacity for evil, they also share a capacity for good" (68). That Miller can, in the midst of dramatizing the horrors of internment and persecution, reveal the crystalline flame of goodness within Fania Fénelon or John Proctor inspires hope.

Fania relentlessly effaces her inner aggression to compete, whether it's for food or affection. All aggression is ultimately tinged with that first active emotion, hatred. In some theories, recognition of the other is considered powerful enough to put restraints on aggression. A good example of such a belief would be the theory of Adam Smith's "invisible hand" (30). In our acquisitive drive to gain more for oneself, Smith argues, each worker intuits that he needs the other to sustain the market economy, and therefore governmental regulations are unnecessary because workers will restrain from destroying each other, since it would not be in each one's best self-interest. This theory places tremendous confidence in the idea that repression has been successfully internalized as super-ego. It is true that in the animal kingdom, creatures will fight over territory, but rarely to the death. In the human world, however, most of us who believe in regulation want to look up and see an objective judge on the bench, and, like Quentin in *After the Fall* (3), we become apprehensive when no authority figure is there to moderate self-other conflicts by serving as a disinterested third to keep overly aggressive forces in check. This stark difference between animal and human violence can only be accounted for by admitting the sickness inherent within human ego.

Like a Buddhist, Fania negates ego. Elzvieta says to Fania, "You are someone to trust, Fania, . . .maybe it's that you have no ideology" (64). The nightmare of the concentration camp is not just that the dominant Nazis have imposed slavery and degradation upon the Jews, but that in the camp itself the mimetic impulse takes over as the prisoners create their own hegemonic microcosm of supremacy with the Poles at the bottom of the prisoner's social order. This sickness to reconstruct hegemony in order to capitalize on someone else's humiliation so as to construct a social identity is a tendency that Fania abhors. Fania longs to avoid this internal pecking order, but of course she cannot. By joining the orchestra, she accumulates to herself certain advantages that elevate her above others who are targeted as candidates for the oven. In one of her interviews with Alma, the great violinist and women's orchestra leader, Fania breaks down because one of the other prisoners has spat on Fania (35). The other prisoners know that the musicians curry favor by performing for the Nazis. The prisoners can only express extreme resentment to the point of spitting. Fania confesses to Alma: "I hadn't realized. . .how they must hate us" (35). Alma, by contrast, has recoiled into her ego, and will only see the world in terms of her egotistic binary: "Fania, there is life or death in this place" (35). This viewpoint resonates with the extreme binary in *The Crucible* expressed by Danforth when he proclaims, ". . .a person is either with this court or he must be counted against it, there be no road between" (87). This divide always presupposes a privileged certitude not open for debate. Opposition becomes a target for exclusion and hatred. Intolerance toward the other echoes as a repetition of early childhood resentment toward the invasive paternal figure. The ego unchained reacts to confrontation with a sense of murderous rage.

Hegemony is a concept closely associated with power. "Hegemon"—we should recall—is the Greek word for *leader*, and when an organization demands extreme leadership, the stage is set for a dictator to assume control. Freud explains in *Group Psychology* how the "hegemon" perpetuates his mystique by evoking libidinal impulses associated with power. The leader becomes an ego ideal. The most effective way for a tyrant to gain sway over the primal horde involves an understanding of how hatred underlies all uncritical idealization. Freud emphasizes this point a number of times in explaining how libidinous excess blinds to the point that "a group. . . has no critical faculty" (78). The "hegemon," therefore, must incite violent energy but deflect it away from himself and onto a scapegoat who has been depicted as demonic. For Hitler, the scapegoat was the Jews; for the Puritans, the scapegoat was the witches.

To grasp hegemony in *The Crucible*, the key figure for us to focus upon is Hale. At the outset Hale shows the same self-centered assurance that we will eventually see manifested to an extreme degree in Danforth. Hale is described as "the specialist" (31) who sees himself as indispensable in ailing the woes of others. The one redeeming positive about Hale is foreshadowed in the stage notes when Miller attributes to him a "searching scrutiny" in examining evidence (31). We are told that Hale had once stood down a town ready to hang a person accused of witchcraft when he exposed the woman as a charlatan. Unlike the despotically confident Danforth, Hale can suspend judgment about appearance to analyze what has been concealed. He has some independent sense of an analytic method not at the mercy of the crowd's blood-lust. Hale becomes what James J. Martine calls a "dynamic" character transformed from "complete intellectual" into a humbled man whose "sense of his own guilt fathers his awareness" (55). But Hale has his limits. Unlike Giles Corey, Hale remains in the dark concerning what Miller calls the "land-lust" that impels Thomas Putnam (7). Unlike John Proctor, Hale cannot grasp how Abigail's predatory vengeance fuels her need to destroy her rival, Elizabeth Proctor. Despite these economic and sexual blind spots, Hale comes to represent, in the final act of the play, the voice of reason by making a concerted effort to uncover the truth. Stephen Marino cites Act Two, the scene where Elizabeth is arrested, as the moment when he believes that Hale first awakens to how the conflict has become about power, with truth being annulled.

Marino finds this moment significant for how Hale reaches a "realization that the weight of the court is now outweighing the weight of his authority" (491). One can also discern a similar awareness taking form in the recent Introduction to the new Penguin edition of *The Crucible*, when Christopher Bigsby stresses, several times, how the play deals with struggles to maintain communal order. However, a subtle shift occurs with the following touchstone sentence: "The question is not the reality of the witches but the power of authority to define the nature of the real, and the desire, on the part of individuals and the state, to identify those whose purging will relieve a sense of anxiety and guilt" (xi). Hale finds himself in a situation where he no longer is capable of standing down a town. Salem has reached a point where the tide of libidinous aggression has risen, and the people are prepared to listen, not to reason, but to the one who will provide an outlet for collective hysteria. Hale does not quite understand the various lusts that can efface reason, but he does realize that the situation is beyond his powers to assert a dispassionate perspective. Since hegemony depends upon maintaining power over the libidinal constitution of the group, the primal horde dictates that the so-called "real" must now be defined, or rather satisfied, at the narcissistic level of sadism, because the mob's binding hatred has reached such a frenzy that the only resolution can come from purgation; hence, we have the sickness that demands a scapegoat.

My reading is that Hale stands up for tolerance, but it would appear that Miller is not quite as taken with this character. In the stage notes, Miller writes, "Better minds than Hale's were—and still are—convinced that there is a society of spirits beyond our ken" (31). I find this observation to constitute a perplexity open to several interpretations. On the one hand, the sentence may urge that we see Hale as a man who did not do nearly enough to oppose the witch-hunt. Indeed, the credit that many attribute to him for trying to save the day can be explained away by claiming that he acts not on behalf of others, but out of solipsism in wishing to save his own soul. On the other hand, I am willing to allow that Hale makes what appears to be a serious effort to save lives. He is no Pontius Pilate, washing his hands of a mob affair over which he has little influence. Hale returns to Salem because he listens to his guilt and assumes responsibility for John Proctor, more responsibility than Proctor's own wife. Hale experiences an enormous fear, envisioning the blood of Proctor on his hands. Hale responds the only way he knows how, by becoming an advocate. The others respond with accusation. Pure hatred inspires no other response than accusation leveled at the one who is marked for exclusion.

At the beginning of *Oedipus Rex*, a plague has swept across the land infecting the society on a cosmic scale. This same proportion is mirrored in *The Crucible*, when Hale warns Danforth:

> Excellency, there are orphans wandering from house to house; abandoned cattle bellow on the highroads, the stink of rotting crops hangs everywhere, and no man knows when the harlots' cry will end his life—and you wonder yet if rebellion's spoke? Better you should marvel how they do not burn your province! (121)

Social malady has infected the entire world, and this sickness can best be seen in the impulse to accuse. From the beginning of the play, Proctor has been the target of an incredible series of accusations. Some of this, Proctor brings on himself, being described in the stage notes as a man who has "a sharp and biting way with hypocrites" (19). Proctor's own arrogant sense of independence opens him up to become a target for resentment. But in no way does this justify the litany of accusations against Proctor that dominate the play. Abby accuses Proctor of being incapable of not wanting her (21–22). Parris accuses Proctor of being an infidel for not attending service (27). Corey gloats about how he had won his case against Proctor, by proving Proctor guilty of defamation (30). Putnam accuses Proctor of stealing wood from his land (30). Of course, Elizabeth will eventually join this long line, accusing her husband of having betrayed their sacred bond (59). If ever a character were foreshadowed as a scapegoat, it is John Proctor.

Danforth will ultimately represent the "hegemon" who deflects anger away from himself and onto Proctor as sacrificial fall guy. In Act Four, Hale warns Danforth that it is a wonder that the mob has not yet come to "burn your province" (121). This choice of words suggests that Hale did not grasp the significance, in Act Three, of Proctor's rant to Danforth: "A fire, a fire is burning! . . .God damns our kind especially, and we will burn, we will burn together!" (111). The thematic implication is abundantly clear: when the entire social order is permeated with unadulterated evil, everyone must be held accountable. No one sacrifice can cure a sickness that has become endemic through ego and accusation run amok. In Freud's one hopeful moment in *Group Psychology*, he urges that "love alone acts as the civilizing factor in the sense that it brings a change from egoism to altruism" (103). *The Crucible* is a world almost devoid of love. Whatever love John Proctor has for others, he is in much the same position as Fania in *Playing for Time*. Neither one is able to connect with another and merge identities through a process that engenders altruism. Yet they each long to do so.

The dénouement in *The Crucible* involves Danforth and Hathorne pushing a pattern of accusation against Proctor to its inevitable conclusion. The intensity of the accusations, totally devoid of reason, exist in what Miller once described as a "mirage world" sustained by the "fundamental absurdity" (284) of "spectral evidence" ("*The Crucible* in History" 289). This insanity awakens Hale to Proctor's innocence. The intensity of charges, fueled by an underlying hatred aimed at Proctor, leads Hale to his perception that Proctor must be innocent. But it's too late to reason with the collective libido that has invested itself in a totalitarian hegemony. In egotism's sadistic binary of Master–Slave, Proctor is positioned to be the weak one who must be sacrificed. Without a dispassionate third who is empowered to question both sides, the master will have his pound of flesh.

The play ends with Proctor being given an impossible choice: if he declares his identification with the devil, he will be granted his life; if he refuses the offer, he will die. Saint Augustine once proclaimed that "an unjust law is no law at all." This realization would seem to justify Proctor's recanting in order to save himself; however, the absence of any law at all in Salem is the real dilemma. There is no escape from the endemic sickness that infects this entire world where accusation makes its own law. The absence of law itself becomes the very factor that motivates Proctor to ascend the gallows. Only by following his own conscience can Proctor establish a norm that has the categorical *weight* of law. We should remember that in Jacques Lacan's rewriting of psychoanalysis, he transforms Freud's concept of the super-ego into what Lacan calls "the Name-of-the-Father"—a concept which "sustains the structure of desire with the structure of the law" (34). With this revised concept, Lacan explains how maturation depends upon transferring the child's sense of love away from maternal assimilation and transferring hatred away from paternal intervention. According to Lacan, the social and symbolic controls function by providing an entire set of sublimations and competitions more healthy than fixation upon a dyadic binary become internecine rivalry. Proctor acknowledges the import of the social order when he declares: "How may I live without my name? I have given you my soul; leave me my name!" (133). Proctor's reason for refusing to sign a false confession is that he loves his children: "I have three children—how may I teach them to walk like men in the world, and I sold my friends?" (132). In refusing to sign his name to a lie, Proctor establishes his name as something more valuable than the libidinous insistence of the horde. The ultimate truth—to which *The Crucible* attests—establishes how parents must love their children out of altruism. Giles Corey chooses to die in order to ensure that he can give to his children the gift of his land. John Proctor then turns Giles into his paternal role model. Giles's assertion of conscience becomes the law of altruism for Proctor who chooses to die in order to ensure that he can give to his children the gift of "the Name-of-the-Father." Proctor calls the court's bluff, much as did Socrates, the father of philosophy, in choosing to drink the hemlock. Giles Corey and John Proctor take a final step beyond Hale's development: they act on their conscience. Without conscience, there can be no responsibility for the other. Without responsibility for the other, there can be no altruism. And without the law of altruism, there can be no community.

Works Cited

Abbotson, Susan C.W. "Re-Visiting the Holocaust for 1980's Television: Arthur Miller's *Playing for Time.*" *American Drama* 8 (1999): 61–78.

Bauman, Zygmunt. *Liquid Modernity.* Cambridge, England: Polity 2000.

Bigsby, Christopher. Introduction to *The Crucible*, by Arthur Miller. New York: Penguin, 2003.

Cook, Kimberly, K. "Self-Preservation in Arthur Miller's Holocaust Dramas." *Journal of Evolutionary Psychology* 14 (1993): 99–108.

Fénelon, Fania. *Playing for Time.* 1976. Translated by Judith Landry. Syracuse: Syracuse University Press, 1997.

Freud, Sigmund. *Civilization and its Discontents.* 1929. *Standard Edition* 21. Translated by James Strachey. London: Hogarth, 1961. 59–145.

———. *Group Psychology and the Analysis of the Ego.* 1921. *Standard Edition* 18. Translated by James Strachey. London: Hogarth, 1955. 69–143.

———. *Totem and Taboo.* 1913. *Standard Edition* 13. Translated by James Strachey. London: Hogarth, 1955. 1–161.

Girard, René. *I See Satan Fall Like Lightning*. Translated by James
    G. Williams. Maryknoll, NY: Orbis, 2001.
———. *Violence and the Sacred*. Translated by Patrick Gregory.
    Baltimore: Johns Hopkins University Press, 1977.
Gottfried, Martin. *Arthur Miller: His Life and Work*. Cambridge,
    MA: Da Capo, 2003.
Halio, Jay L. "Arthur Miller's Broken Jews." In *American Literary
    Dimensions: Poems and Essays in Honor of Melvin J. Friedman*.
    Edited by Ben Siegel and Jay L. Halio. Newark, NJ: University
    of Delaware Press, 1999. 128–35.
Lacan, Jacques. *The Four Fundamental Concepts of Psycho-Analysis*.
    Edited by Jacques-Alain Miller. Translated by Alan Sheridan.
    New York: Norton, 1981.
Marino, Stephen. "Arthur Miller's 'Weight of Truth' in *The
    Crucible*." In *Modern Critical Interpretations: Arthur Miller* The
    Crucible. Edited by Harold Bloom. New York: Chelsea House,
    1999. 177–85. First published in *Modern Drama* 38 (1995): 488–
    95.
Martine, James J. The Crucible: *Politics, Property, and Pretense*.
    New York: Twayne, 1993.
Miller, Arthur. *After the Fall*. 1963. New York: Penguin, n.d.
———. "Clinton in Salem." *Echoes Down the Corridor: Collected
    Essays — 1944–2000*. Edited by Steven R. Centola. New York:
    Viking, 2000. 267–69.
———. *The Crucible*. 1953. New York: Penguin, 2003.
———. "*The Crucible* in History." *Echoes Down the Corridor:
    Collected Essays — 1944–2000*. Edited by Steven R. Centola.
    New York: Viking, 2000. 274–95.
———. *Death of a Salesman*. 1949. New York: Penguin, n.d.
———. *Playing for Time*. 1980. Screenplay. *Plays: (Volume) Two*.
    New York: Methuen, 1994. 447–531.
———. *Playing for Time*. Stage play. Woodstock, IL: Dramatic
    Publishing Company, 1985.
Ricoeur, Paul. "The Demythization of Accusation." *The Conflict of
    Interpretation*. Edited by Don Ihde. Translated by Peter
    McCormick. Evanston: Northwestern University Press, 1974.
    335–53.
Santayana, George. *The Life of Reason*. Volume 1: *Reason in
    Common Sense*. New York: Scribner's, 1905.
Smith, Adam. *The Wealth of Nations*. Volume 2. Edited by Edwin
    Cannan. New Rochelle, NY: Arlington, 1966.

Arthur Miller's *Clara*: An Interrogation of Middle American Political Correctness

Paula T. Langteau

In 1986, Arthur Miller wrote a short play, *Clara*, about the aftermath of a gruesome deed: the brutal murder of Clara Kroll. The entire focus of the one-act play is the interrogation by detective Lew Fine of Clara's father, Albert Kroll, who, having just found his daughter's decapitated corpse in the adjoining room, awakens from fainting as the play opens. Fine's purpose is to uncover some clue as to who the murderer might be, and throughout the play, he questions Kroll to this end. The conflict arises with Kroll's inability to provide the name of the main suspect, Clara's Hispanic ex-convict lover, without coming to terms with the part his own values, values which he instilled in Clara, played in bringing about her death. And, only when he confronts those values by reliving scenes from the past can Kroll assist the detective. The detective facilitates that necessary confrontation through his effective, albeit harsh, interrogation strategy. As David Savran explains, "Kroll, . . .tortured by his inability to remember his daughter's lover, needs to be broken down by the detective, who, using a Freudian stratagem (based on the assumption that "we block things we're ashamed to remember"), makes Kroll first confess to his own guilt in the belief that this will remove the obstacle" (73). The tactic works. But ultimately the play is not so much about the detective's interrogation technique as it is about what it is Kroll must confess to and the question of his guilt. What are the values that he passed on to his daughter? and do they indict him in Clara's death?

Miller, in his autobiography *Timebends*, suggests that "Kroll. . .had handed Clara some of his own early idealism as she grew up" (590) an idealism which, Miller claims, made Kroll "what Whitman might have thought of as one of his 'Democratic men'" (591). The problem, according to Miller, is that "in the past twenty years Kroll has changed" (591). Miller explains:

> Not that he has become a bad man but simply that the ideal has flown. . . .[I]n this bloodied room where his daughter died[,] [however,] he is confronted with the ideal again. Must he disown it, suffer guilt and remorse for having misled his child? Or, despite everything, confirm the validity of the ideal and his former trust in mankind, in effect keeping faith with the best in himself, accepting the tragedy of her sacrifice to what he once again sees was and is worth everything?" (590-91).

Steven Centola and Terry Otten also describe Kroll as "an essentially good person who lost his faith in the goodness of humanity" (Otten 206), a man whose early values they consider "liberal" (Centola 63), who now, later in life, has "sold out" (Otten 206) his ideal, a process that, "however unintentionally, [makes him]… responsible for Clara's death" (Otten 206). Terry Otten asserts that "Clara had embodied her father's commitment to social justice and reform" (205), and Centola suggests that Clara's adoption of that commitment—those liberal values—as her own "may have led indirectly to her death" (63-64). True, Kroll's values, which Clara does adopt as her own, *do* indict him in Clara's death, but a careful interrogation of them reveals that what makes them dangerous is not that they are "liberal," reflective of a commitment to social justice, or some earlier (though now departed) idealism, but that they are, and seem always to have been, superficial, based upon assumptions and stereotypes of people rather than on distinct individuals.

The audience gains a glimpse into the values Kroll has passed on to his daughter through scenes from the past that intrude upon his present consciousness. In particular, in an onstage flashback, Kroll recounts telling Clara two stories of "heroism" which deeply move the impressionable young woman. In the first, he describes being "jumped" (54) in the Philippines in a Japanese surprise attack during WWII. In defense of his life, Kroll describes how he "grabbed that Japanese and bent him over his knees till [he] broke his back" (55). Clara interprets the act as resulting from what she calls "the strength of rage" (55) and casts the act in a positive light since she believes in the goodness of her father, who is not otherwise a killer. This interpretation becomes dangerous for her, however, when she aligns it with her lover's "illusion that he was defending his life" (55) when he murdered his former girlfriend, a crime for which he served about ten years in prison (46). When Clara equates both her father's and her lover's taking of a life to "that same uncontrollable rage" (54), she indirectly equates the men in general as well, causing her to conclude that her lover, like her father, will not kill again. She insists, "He'll never have that illusion again, Papa" (55). By generalizing the act of killing—whether in war or in a violent domestic crime—and categorizing together the men who do the killing, Clara not only diminishes the severity of her lover's crime but she assigns to him the same goodness and heroism she sees in her father.

Clara's belief in her father's goodness derives directly from the second story, which he told her much earlier, when she was "a young girl" (65). Reliving the scene, Kroll relates how, as an officer in the "still segregated army" (65), he volunteered to take command of an all black company that, he says, "nobody wanted" (66) and that the colonel was unwilling to assist when a "lynching mob" began "chasing them through Biloxi" (66). In a heroic account that mesmerizes and strikes awe in the young Clara, Kroll describes how he drove into Biloxi and, upon seeing

> a mob with half a dozen of my guys, some of them already [with] ropes around their necks[,]. . . . I jumped up onto the hood of the jeep and took out my .45 and fired it into the air[,]. . . . [calling out], "I am an officer of the United States Army! Now you untie my men and hand them over to me right now!" (66-67)

This action saved the lives of the soldiers. Kroll remembers,

> And. . .my God, I couldn't believe it. . .one by one they let them out of the crowd. Nobody touched them, and three or four got into the jeep and the rest lay flat on the hood and some stood on the bumpers and we drove down Main Street and out of town. (67)

Scholars have focused on this passage as evidence of Kroll's liberal values, "his commitment to human rights and social equality [that] was firmly and deeply instilled in his daughter" (Centola, "Temporality" 140), considering it "his greatest moment of moral courage and conviction" (Otten 208), "the moment. . .that gave [Clara] the uncompromising idealism that led to her death" (Otten 207). Miller himself suggests that this recollection is important because it awakens in Kroll a recognition that "in the past twenty years [he] has changed. . .the ideal has flown" (591), while it had remained alive in his daughter. Centola explains,

> As [Kroll] finishes his story and remembers receiving a kiss from his proud daughter, he sees clearly his complicity in her death. Her admiration of her father and respect for his values led to her work first in the Peace Corps and then later in prison rehabilitation—a career that unfortunately involved her in a romance with the convicted murderer who would ultimately kill her. ("Temporality" 140)

Since Kroll's psychological obstacle to remembering the full name of Clara's lover, Luis Hernandez, is removed upon the retelling of this story, the assumption is that in retelling it, Kroll "confirm[s] the validity of [his earlier] ideal[s]. . .,accepting the tragedy of [Clara's] sacrifice to what he once again sees was and is worth everything" (Miller 591), and, as a result, becomes able to name the suspect. As Centola explains it, "Kroll comes to accept his culpability without abandoning his social responsibility. He chooses to embrace his life even though he knows doing so necessitates accepting the tragedy of Clara's sacrifice" (*Conversation* 64).

This conclusion, however, does not provide a resolution to the clear cognitive dissonance between an apparent reaffirmation of Kroll's seemingly internalized liberal social values and an acceptance of their very immediate deadly consequences. In fact, a few of the play's early reviewers quite compellingly conclude that recognition of such dissonance leads to the opposite of a recommitment to social equality and an embracing of life. William A. Henry of *Time* contends that Kroll, "a man about Miller's age[,] admits that after basing his life on progressive principles, he is no longer sure these tenets do the world any good" (88), and Robert Brustein, writing for *The New Republic*, wonders, "Is [Miller saying] that the thing preventing Kroll from naming names is his liberalism, his sympathy for the underprivileged, and that he cannot identify his daughter's killer until he understands how such ideas have indirectly caused her death" (26)? If this is the case, it would follow, as Brustein concludes, that "his grief will most likely destroy his vulnerable spirit along with his liberal convictions" (26). But this is not the case. The problem with these readings is that Kroll's "ideals" and "values" have not been defined in them. Those so-called "liberal convictions" must be interrogated.

To begin with, let's return to the two stories. In each of the stories, Kroll confronts the racial Other, whether in the form of the Japanese enemy or the African-American soldier, as *representation* rather than as *individual*. While in the first story Kroll's impulse is to kill and in the second it is to save, he similarly distances himself from the Other by referring to *them* as types rather than human beings. This distancing serves not only to make the Other less human than he is but allows him to cast himself as heroic in comparison. *That* so-called heroism, and not any true liberalism, is what Clara emulates.

In his recollection of Biloxi, Kroll tells Clara he volunteered to command the company of black soldiers because "Grandpa'd always had Negro people in the nursery and, you know—I'd been around them all my life and always got along with them" (66), though in an earlier scene he confides to the detective, "[T]ell you the truth, every once in a while I just about give up on those people" (51), a result of having had, in his own words, "more than the usual amount of experience with them" (52). It takes just a small step to go from this kind of typing of "those people" to the utter dehumanizing Kroll exhibits in his description of the Japanese in their surprise attack on him: "I was fast asleep in the tent," he tells Clara, "and suddenly they were all over me like roaches" (54).

Indeed Kroll's typing of people pervades the play. When Fine asks him how his wife reacted to meeting Luis—"this Puerto Rican in a windbreaker" (51), as Fine calls him—Kroll responds matter-of-factly, "Jean was a Rockette" as if the link between ideas should be obvious: he tells Fine, "they're accustomed to associating with all kinds of people in show business" (51). So, Luis is not treated as an individual; he is a Puerto Rican who, like African-Americans, Japanese, and even Rockettes, can be neatly categorized by the *kind of people they are*, and, by extension, by the way *those kind of people* act and the way *those kind of people* think.

Typing, as a big issue, exerts itself most symbolically in the play through the character of Lew Fine. First, the detective has experienced typing, and its natural companion *discrimination*, as a Jew taking his sergeant's exam, a story he recounts to Kroll. Further, and more importantly, he represents a *type* that Kroll can identify in his former friend, Bert, whose last name, not coincidentally, is Fine as well. The two Fines share an amazing set of characteristics: Lew is "almost the spitting image" of Bert (36), both lost toes on their left feet during the war (42), and both had sons who commit suicide during Vietnam (43). As the detective explains it to Kroll, "Our statistics probably crossed, your friend [Bert] and I, it's bound to happen somewhere on the graph" (43). More revealingly, however, he adds, "We're all one step away from a statistic" (43), a comment that suggests not only the potential dehumanizing of *all* "kinds of people" but also, ultimately, the kind of deadly statistic that brings detectives into homes to interrogate fathers.

The irony to Kroll's typing of people, however, is that it causes him to become *Other* to himself because he is alien to his own native bigotry. In fact, Kroll causes himself to believe that his typing of people (which creates class as well as racial categories) is not just innocuous but actually beneficial. As chairman of the zoning board he acts with perfect political correctness in resisting the "terrific pressure" (59) he claims he has been under to raise the acreage requirement for building houses, a measure designed "to keep out less affluent families" (60). But the language he uses to describe his actions—referring to the less affluent as "them"—reflects an underlying categorizing of people: He tells Fine, "We've got to let them in. I don't know what else to support. Or you end up with two societies" (60). Thus, his "good deeds" on the one hand conflict with his underlying prejudices on the other.

The suppressed internal conflict of not truly believing what he has taught Clara indicts Kroll, at a subconscious level, for his daughter's death. And it is only when he admits that his so-called heroism "was nothing" (67), that his exercising of liberal values has been a performance in which he cast himself not only as *separate* and *superior* but also as *savior* to the Other, that he remembers Luis' last name. The text indicates Kroll comes to a "double awareness" (67) as he tries to dissuade Clara from idolizing him for intervening in the attempted lynching of his black company. He becomes aware of his two selves— the politically correct surface self and the underlying bigot. He recognizes that he, like Luis, suppresses "the same uncontrollable rage," as Clara calls it. While Luis' rage seems to be directed toward women, Kroll's targets particular ethnic groups, social classes and even sexual orientations. And while for Luis the rage burst forth into at least one (that we know of) extreme violent physical act (because, despite circumstantial evidence, he still has a right to a fair trail for Clara's murder), for Kroll it seeps out insidiously into his conversations and behaviors.

The sudden "double awareness" indicates Kroll's recognition of how those suppressed values implicate him in Clara's death. He recognizes, as Fine points out to him, "It's ten, twenty, thirty years of shit you told your daughter, to the point where she sacrificed her life, for what?" (61). For what, indeed? Perhaps to make her father proud? She did choose to work in the Peace Corp and later in prison rehabilitation, and in these choices she wins a reciprocal admiration from her father like that which she showed to him for his seemingly heroic acts. This is depicted in the play in Kroll's recollection of an incident that happened during a riot at Botsford Penitentiary while Clara worked there. Kroll recounts how "they held her hostage, had a knife to her jugular. *[And, at this point, the text indicates that he laughs.]* And when it was over, [Kroll says,] she went right back in" (46). The detective, who doesn't seem to find the story amusing, points out to Kroll, ". . .[D]eep down you were proud of her doing that, right?" (46) But what is it Kroll is proud of? What is it that makes him *laugh*? Her social commitment? Or, is he proud that his daughter, like him, has taken on a larger-than-life stature, casting herself as superior to *those people,* as their savior, the invincible hero who comes to their rescue? She has not only accepted her father's values but she has successfully emulated him in her posture toward *those people* as well.

The recognition of the implications of what he has taught her comes hard to Kroll. Unlike with the lynching mob and the rioting prisoners, this time the hero does not escape unscathed. Here in her living room, with her lifeless, decapitated body lying in an adjoining room, Kroll sees so clearly the horrible truth of his culpability. As Miller puts it, "Kroll finds himself having to confront her idealism, which now looms as the path to her death since she persisted in working with ex-prison inmates to *save them* for *useful lives* [my emphasis]" (590). And, as Savran carefully ascertains, "In an almost expressionistic manner, the intersection of remembrance and confession configures the murderer not as a distinct entity but as an Other within the self, as a man who, despite his superficial differences from Kroll, becomes his fantasmatic double" (74). Kroll sees the suppressed "Other" within himself as the murderer who takes Clara's life.

The problem with Kroll's seemingly "liberal values" (and what proves deadly in them for Clara) is that they are worn much like he senses Luis wears his association with Clara, "like a medal. . .on his chest. . . .like an accomplishment for him" (55). They don't penetrate beyond a surface categorizing of people, a surface political correctness disguising underlying prejudice and, in fact, an opportunity for self-aggrandizement. Because he cannot distinguish between the type and the individual, he cannot convey to Clara that while "most of the Puerto Rican people don't become criminals" (54), Luis Hernandez, as an individual, has proven to be dangerous; that while the zoning board "could easily get sued by the federal government for housing discrimination if [they] go to four acres" (60), Clara should not live, as she did, with only a single lock on her door (38), in a neighborhood in which "she has been robbed once before" (37). For Kroll, and subsequently for Clara, the granting of equality to groups necessitates the denying of the equality of the individual. The notion of the group is monolithic; it cannot afford individuals. To name the individual is to destroy the idealism of a categorically sympathetic response to the group. Thus, Kroll's overwhelming guilt is that to name Hernandez, for him, is to name Puerto Ricans, causing him to deny the seemingly politically correct values he has taught Clara.

Worse, Kroll's typing of people, with its accompanying prejudice, causes him to prefer one type over another regardless of the individuals represented, placing him in a position of condoning the potentially dangerous while ruling out the potentially beneficial. He tells the detective about his visiting Clara one evening while she was entertaining a social psychologist co-worker and witnessing, through Clara's apartment window, Clara kissing the woman goodnight. For that reason, Kroll failed to intervene in Clara's relationship with Luis because, as Fine so aptly puts it, "it was such a relief to see her involved with a man . . .even a Puerto Rican murderer" (59) that he said and did nothing to oppose the relationship. Thus categories, or types, become hierarchically rank-ordered, with "Homosexual" clearly falling below both "Puerto Rican" and "Known Criminal."

In the final analysis, then, Kroll's values indict him in his daughter's death not because they're liberal but because they're a facade: while they exhibit a surface political correctness they are based upon assumptions and stereotypes about categories of people rather than on behaviors of, and experience with, distinct individuals. Clara's death (and Fine's interrogation) force Kroll to reexamine these false liberal values to determine their validity in relation to the life they've claimed. Perhaps, as Miller asserts, Kroll *is* "confronted with. . .the ideal" (591), but it seems clear that it is an ideal that he has not confronted before but only mimicked in a distant and shadowy distortion of social political correctness. Ultimately, Kroll must come to terms with the suppressed internal conflict of not truly embracing the idealism behind his seemingly politically correct posturing, a posturing that Clara had emulated (and which clearly jeopardized her safety), which indicts him, at a subconscious level, for his daughter's death. He is confronted with the opportunity to realize the true ideal only in light of the horrifying consequences of the false values by which he raised Clara.

In a contemporary America overwrought with racism, classism and homophobia, and in the face of pressure to do what is right with regard to the Other—granting full rights to all people—Miller's play points out the dangers of settling for a politically correct posture that does not penetrate underlying values. In *Clara*, he challenges us to ask: What are *truly* "liberal" values? How do we, as a country, get beyond our categorizing and typing of people? Can we translate politically correct attitudes into action on an *individual* level? How do we protect ourselves from danger without succumbing to prejudice and paranoia? And, finally, what are the consequences of our failure to open a discourse about who and what is really dangerous?

Works Cited

Brustein, Robert. "Danger: Manipulation." *The New Republic* 196 (9 Mar. 1987): 26.

Centola, Steven R. *Arthur Miller in Conversation*. Dallas: Northouse and Northouse, 1993.

———. "Temporality, Consciousness and Transcendence in *Danger: Memory!*" In *The Achievement of Arthur Miller: New Essays*. Edited by Steven R. Centola. Dallas: Contemporary Research Press, 1995. 135-42.

Henry, William A. "Cry from the Heart." *Time* 129 (9 Mar. 1987): 88.

Otten, Terry. *The Temptation of Innocence in Dramas of Arthur Miller*. Columbia: University of Missouri Press, 2002.

Miller, Arthur. *Clara*. In *Danger: Memory!* New York: Grove, 1986. 31-68.

————. *Timebends: A Life*. New York: Grove, 1987.

Savran, David. *Communists, Cowboys and Queers: The Politics of Masculinity in the Work of Arthur Miller and Tennessee Williams.* Minneapolis: University of Minnesota Press, 1992.

"Physician Heal Thyself": Arthur Miller's Portrayal of Doctors

Stephen A. Marino

In *The Temptation of Innocence in the Dramas of Arthur Miller*, Terry Otten points out how any reader of Miller knows that his work is filled with references to jail, crime, and the law (16). Consequently, many of his plays contain lawyers as both major and minor characters. Of course, the most notable examples are George Deever in *All My Sons*, Bernard in *Salesman*, Danforth in *The Crucible*, Alfieri in *A View From the Bridge*, Quentin in *After the Fall*, and Tom Wilson in *The Ride Down Mt. Morgan*. These attorneys have been the subject of significant critical scrutiny which focuses on their action as conduits to the moral truth that the particular play illustrates.

Although Neil Carson has written that the professional class in Miller's plays is represented almost exclusively by lawyers (153), Miller also has filled his plays with a substantial number of doctors. And unlike the somewhat consistent depiction of lawyers as moral arbiters, Miller's physicians often have personal conflicts which impinge upon their professional lives. Some are trusted by their patients; others doubted; one approaches a violation of his Hippocratic Oath. Most have difficulty, certainly much more than Miller's lawyers, in discerning the relevance of truth for themselves. Miller's doctors are often misguided; their moral centers are unclear, askew. Their ethics are sometimes questionable. Most importantly, their roles as healers are in direct conflict with their personal desires. Thus, they seem most conflicted by their personal and public roles, and, therefore, their debt to the self and society, struggles which are, as Miller himself consistently has pointed out, at the center of all the great plays. All Miller doctors confront his great themes of public vs. private guilt and responsibility; however, their role as doctors and healers complicate the tension between these. Yet, many of them are often crucial in the resolution of conflict.

From Jim Bayliss in Miller's first Broadway hit, *All My Sons* to Harry Hyman in *Broken Glass*, the large number of physicians (equal to or even greater than the number of attorneys) have played significant roles in Arthur Miller's dramatic canon as both major, minor, and even absent characters. These physicians also cover a wide range of specialties in the medical profession: Jim Bayliss is a general practitioner, a family doctor of the small Midwestern town where *All My Sons* takes place; Thomas Stockmann in *An Enemy of the People* is a self-described doctor/scientist; Walter in *The Price* is a surgeon, LeDuc in *Incident at Vichy* is a psychiatrist; Harry Hyman is an internist, dabbling in psychiatry, outside his field.

Steve Centola has described Jim Bayliss as a character who is escaping from reality (58). In an interview with Chris Bigsby, Arthur Miller described Harry Hyman as a "scientific idealist" (180). What every Miller doctor possesses in common is an idealism that clashes with reality. Most often their idealism—whether in their professional or personal lives—thrusts them into a conflict with forces of society which temper their idealism—leaving them forever changed in the process. Most importantly, their medical ethics complicate their decision making. Perhaps Miller's doctors are most conflicted by LeDuc's self-analysis at the end of *Incident at Vichy*: "In my profession one gets the habit of looking at oneself quite impersonally" (65), and they, therefore, have difficulty handling personal conflicts or confrontation.

Perhaps the prototypical Miller doctor is the minor character Dr. Jim Bayliss in *All My Sons* because he typifies the conflict between idealism and reality that is evident in all of Miller's doctors. Jim Bayliss also is a fitting character to begin this discussion since *All My Sons* apparently takes place in America's heartland, perhaps Ohio, and Bayliss is somewhat representative of the small-town American middle class practitioner. What is striking about him is that he challenges the complacency of his Midwestern values.

Bayliss primarily functions in the play as contrast to Chris Keller, who, in the main plot of the drama, comes to an awareness of his father Joe Keller's guilt and cover-up in the manufacturing and selling of defective airplane parts during WWII, acts which resulted in fatal plane crashes. Chris's own idealist outlook is jolted when he fully comprehends the reality of his father's complicity in the deaths of twenty-one pilots. Miller depicts Bayliss as having had a similar struggle of idealism vs. reality, but we do not witness this in the play—it has occurred years before—and Bayliss primarily gives reflection on Chris's confrontation. However, the play details significant information about Jim's previous struggle, and it is crucial that the personal crisis in his life arose from his attitude toward the medical profession. In fact, the very first scene of the play highlights Jim's dissatisfaction with his chosen profession when he relates to his neighbor that his own son will become a doctor over his "dead body" and he further rejects the judgment that medicine is an "honorable profession."

The initial scene of Act One also depicts how Jim struggles between the noble goal of wanting to "help humanity" and the reality of earning a substantial living for his family as a small town doctor. In fact, the play illustrates much of this through the constant haranguing of his wife Sue who complains both about the money Jim earns and his female patients' attention to him. Sue, a former nurse, is even described by Joe Keller as being "too realistic," as a counter to Jim's idealism. In act two Sue's complaints are clearly evident in her conversation with Ann Deever, Chris's fiancée. Sue knows that although Jim is a successful doctor, he is torn by the desire to do medical research. Sue clearly puts the blame for this on Chris who has infected Jim with what she describes as his "phony idealism" to make Jim feel as if he has compromised himself. Of course, all of this about Jim is true as he himself says in Act Three when Chris has run off after discovering the truth about Joe Keller. Jim tells Kate that Chris eventually will return home and confront the reality of Joe's crime—and he proceeds to relate the crucial moment in his own life when the compromise was made and the "star of [his] honesty" went out: he took off, went to New Orleans, studied a disease—a period of life he describes as "beautiful"—until Sue came crying and he returned home with her to "live in the usual darkness" (74).

This speech by Jim is quite important because we understand how his actions in the play show just how seriously he has compromised his idealism. One can make the argument that Jim, like other Miller doctors, seriously compromises his medical ethics in the play. In Act Two Jim has gone to the station to pick up George Deever who is going to expose the truth of Joe Keller's actions. When Jim returns, wise to George's intentions, he attempts to protect the Kellers from George's accusations. Steve Centola has written that Jim's interference reflects "on his own insecurities and feeble effort to escape from reality" (32). I would argue further that Jim's action is even a violation of medical ethics. In this scene, Jim tells Ann that Kate is in "bad shape" and can not be told the truth. This at first seems merely to be his personal analysis of her emotional condition, but when George enters, he notes, "Doctor said your mother isn't well" (51), clearly indicating that Jim, in the ride back with George, has offered—even concocted—a medical condition or a more severe psychological analysis for Kate than the play has previously documented. Is Jim's devotion to the Kellers so great that he will also compromise his medical oath?

The compromising of medical ethics for an idealized vision is an overlooked aspect of Thomas Stockmann in *Enemy of the People,* the first Miller doctor who is the protagonist of a play. However, Stockmann is included as part of the doctors in Miller's canon with a huge caveat, for Stockmann is not entirely Miller's creation. In 1950 Miller wrote an adaptation—he termed it a "new translation into spoken English" (12)—of Henrik Ibsen's 1882 play, *An Enemy of the People.* The play concerns itself with Thomas Stockmann, a doctor who refuses to allow his town to operate a spa when he discovers the unhealthy quality of the water supply. Stockmann literally becomes the enemy of the townspeople who turn their wrath on him, one of its most respected citizens, because his decision threatens their profit-making ability. Although critics have analyzed the differences between Miller's version and Ibsen's original,[1] some of Stockmann's particular actions as a doctor compare with the actions of Miller's other physicians which he wholly conceived.

Miller describes Stockmann in liner notes as a man who "will not compromise for less than God's own share of the world" (23). Certainly, Stockmann's initial action regarding the health spa is based on his sound medical analysis and principles. He is clearly concerned about the deleterious effect of the infectious organic matter on the visitors to the spa; the typhoid and gastric disturbances are real. He clearly feels a personal and professional responsibility in this regard since he is on the spa's board of directors as medical advisor and he is considered the creator of Kirsten Springs. However, Stockmann's professional and medical responsibilities conflict with the town's business and political interests, and these forces will combine to destroy him and his family. In the crucial conversation with his brother in Act One, a scene in which Peter apparently tries to offer a kind of crooked political compromise, we see how Thomas's uncompromising idealism will bring about his doom. It is interesting that he defends his "convictions" based on his stance as a physician— "I am a doctor and a scientist" (56)—positions which he believes endow him with truth.

There is no doubting, and admiring, Stockmann's steadfast sticking to his convictions even when he knows the literal threat to his family, his house, and his practice. However, Stockmann's medical idealism is somewhat tainted in the play. There are moments where he abandons his medical ethos for what he perceives as greater goods. He clearly possesses radical political ideas and makes alliances with extremists, who abandon him when he, unlike they, refuses to change his convictions. Stockmann's failure is that his political and social idealism compromise his medical ethos. He indicates to Hovstad, Billing, and Alsasken of *The People's Messenger*, the leftist paper that supports his cause, that his drive to clean up the spa will lead to other sociological changes: "This is only the beginning. We'll go on to other subjects and blow up every lie we live by" (66). And flush with this fever, he even abandons a half-bandaged patient in his office. Perhaps Stockmann somewhat resembles Jim Bayliss in that he actually lost a bit of his idealism even before the play begins, when he was living and practicing up north. He compromised himself when he took the financial security offered by his brother in the town.

Miller's 1964 play *Incident at Vichy* also features a doctor who is a significant character in the play and whose decisive action is very much dictated by his medical ethics. *Incident at Vichy* takes place in a room in Vichy, France, during World War II where men suspected of being Jews are detained before questioning; the interrogation determines either their release or further incarceration in a concentration camp. The play details the characters' discussion of the fate that awaits them if they cannot prove their identity papers are valid. Two characters in the play who have received significant critical attention are the Major, a Nazi officer assisting with the roundup, and the gentile Austrian Prince Von Berg who often is seen as the most important character because the drama details his growing awareness of his responsibility as an aristocrat, as a gentile, and as a human being for the atrocities in Europe.

However, the character LeDuc plays a significant role in forcing Von Berg to this realization. LeDuc stands out from Miller's other doctors since he is not strictly a medical doctor but also a practicing psychiatrist. Not only has Martin Roth called LeDuc the leading character, but he has judged that *Incident at Vichy* "corresponds to the analytical process" focusing on the theme of personal responsibility (140). LeDuc's position as a practicing psychiatrist is quite apparent in the action since he deftly examines the motives, drives, wills, and consciences of the other detainees as they sit and wait to be called into the examination. LeDuc probes the men's fears, anxieties, self-doubt, and desire to be free or captured. This is vividly illustrated in his questioning of the painter LeBeau and the actor Monceau about their acceptance, compliance, guilt, and responsibility about being Jewish and victims. He challenges Monceau by suggesting that he wanted to be caught when he left his name in his discarded books and challenges LeBeau by asking him to project how he will act when the examiners demand that he show them his circumcised penis. LeDuc forces each man to realize, "Your heart is conquered territory" (52).

The most important analyses which LeDuc performs are with the Major and Von Berg. His confrontation with Major is quite ironic since they have met before in literal battle at Amiens, where it is suggested the Major was wounded. However, this conflict is now a psychological battlefield. The Major's recovery from the wounded leg prevents him returning to the battlefield, so he has been assigned to the examination of Jews in Vichy, a detail which he admits "takes a little getting used to" (42). LeDuc attempts to examine what he quickly perceives as the Major's humanity and decency. However, the Major exhibits his frustration that every man lacks individual control of his fate in a world at war. Against such forces, the Major wants to maintain his dignity as a "man of honor" (56), but his hunger to survive "other's" sadism is just as strong as any other man's— gentile or Jew—so he does what he must in order to survive and loses his humanity in the process. But in a psychological twist, as he points his gun at LeDuc, the Major forces LeDuc to acknowledge that he too shares this same hunger for self-preservation when Leduc admits that he would not refuse release if the others were kept in custody.

LeDuc's questioning of Von Berg is the climax of the play. What is particularly significant is that as we see with Miller's other doctors, LeDuc also comes to terms with a struggle between idealism and reality. LeDuc forces Von Berg to consider "the price of idealism" in a world which has lost it. As LeDuc says: "And yet can one wish for a world without ideals?" (63) LeDuc makes Von Berg conscious of his lack of personal responsibility for the Holocaust, not because he is anti-Semitic, but because the Jew comes to symbolize "the other," every man his Jew, his psychological other. Von Berg has ignored his cousin's role in the purging of Jewish doctors in Vienna; he has left Austria rather than resist. And in the ultimate irony, Von Berg hands over his pass to LeDuc not out of guilt but out of responsibility to humanity.

LeDuc's struggle between idealism and reality is quite evident in these scenes as he attempts the intellectual and emotional comprehension of the fate that may await him in a gas chamber. As he tells Monceau: "I am being impersonal, as scientific as I know how to be" (49). Perhaps LeDuc is most conflicted by his own self-analysis: "In my profession one gets the habit of looking at oneself quite impersonally" (65)—and has difficulty handling personal conflicts. We see this most vividly when he relates to Von Berg how he was caught by the authorities that morning. How ironic that the doctor himself made a bad *medical* decision when he was caught trying to find codeine to alleviate the pain of his wife's toothache knowing that she would get well eventually.

In 1968 Miller followed *Incident at Vichy* with *The Price* in which he once again employed a doctor as a main character. In this play, he dramatized conflicts he had explored in previous plays—the struggle between two brothers—and themes of personal responsibility and regret. It stands out as the one Miller play between brothers where one is a physician, and the choice of becoming one is arguably the central focus.

The play is about two estranged brothers who meet in the attic of their long deceased father's brownstone, which is being demolished, to settle on a price with an appraiser for its contents. Victor Franz is a police officer who years earlier had given up his dream of becoming a scientist in order to care for his elderly widowed father who had apparently lost everything in the Depression; Walter Franz is a successful surgeon who has forsaken the family for years. During the course of the play, both brothers, along with Victor's wife, battle over their regrets, frustrations, and responsibility for the choices they made years ago—the "price" they now realize they paid. At the climax of the play, Victor blames Walter for not giving him the $500 he needed to finish school and earn his degree. When Walter insists that Victor could have abandoned the father and finished school regardless, Victor rejects that as impossible. Then Walter reveals the huge secret of the play: the father had over $4,000 in savings about which he never told Victor. Moreover, Victor admits he knew that his father was not completely destitute.

Thus, *The Price* explores how both brothers confront their responsibility for decisions they made years ago about their father and each other, and the dramatic tension of the play is how Victor and Walter finally account for those decisions. *The Price* illustrates how one must ultimately face the consequences for past actions. Each brother brings to the attic his version of the past: Walter believes that he actually wished to lend Victor the money, and Victor believes he sacrificed his career to care for the father. Each man has his illusions and rationalizations shattered, and each ultimately comes to understand his personal responsibility.

Much of *The Price* focuses on the medical profession. Although Walter does not appear in the play until the very last moments of act one, he, his career, and lifestyle as a doctor consume much of Victor and Esther's conversation. There is much talk of Walter's financial assets, of which Walter and Esther are obviously resentful because they are clearly struggling financially. Esther especially judges that Walter owes a moral and financial debt to Victor for having taken care of their father because he otherwise would have never been able to finish medical school. Esther even suggests that as a successful research scientist, Walter should be in a position to help Victor start a new career when he retires from the police force. Intriguingly, she describes an idealism that Walter either possesses or once possessed. This reference clearly places Walter in the same situation as Miller's other doctors, for later in Act Two, Walter relates how much he compromised his medical idealism for his lucrative practice.

There is considerable evidence in the play that suggests that Victor wanted to be a doctor or research scientist. We are told that he was brighter than Walter; he was good in science; it was the field he was studying when he had to leave school to care for the father. Victor even is considering another career in the same field. Interestingly, the very attic room in which the play occurs was the former play lab for Victor and Walter when they were young. Ironically the lab was dismantled when Victor and the father moved into the room—a visible reminder of the destruction of Victor's dream of being a scientist.

Act Two clearly illustrates how Walter has indeed compromised his medical idealism throughout his career. In fact, the play blatantly tackles the issue of medical ethics when the ninety year old appraiser, Solomon, compares the ethics of appraisers with those of lawyers and doctors. This occurs just after Walter has told Esther and Victor about the luxurious camel hair coat he has accepted from a wealthy patient for the price of two gallstones. Walter later details how he has compromised his personal life and the professional idealism of his youth by owning lucrative nursing homes, dabbling in the market, and soaking the rich. However, this Walter is the physician of the past. Like Miller's other doctors—Jim Bayliss and Thomas Stockmann—the Walter we see in the play is a man whose ideals have changed. For Walter also details his own illness—apparently a nervous breakdown which caused him to realize the kind of compromised physician he had become:

> You start out wanting to be the best, and there's no question that you do need a certain fanaticism; there's so much to know and so little time.   Until you've eliminated everything extraneous...including people. And of course the time comes when you realize that you haven't been specializing in something—something has been specializing in you. You become a kind of instrument, an instrument that cuts money out of people, or fame out of the world. And it finally makes you stupid. Power can do that. (82)

And of all of Miller's doctors, Walter shows his awareness of the negative and positive aspects of the profession. He says: "All I ever wanted was simply to do science, but I invented an efficient, disaster-proof, moneymaker" (110); "And you end up with the respect, the career, the money, and the best of all, the thing that no body else can tell you so you can believe—that you're one hell of a guy and never harmed anybody in your life!" (111-12); "I worked for what I made and there are people walking around today who'd have been dead if I hadn't" (112-13). However, the change in him is evident when Walter admits: "For the first time. I do medicine" (82). Thus the play elevates from literal physical healing to emotional healing. And Walter—the physician having healed himself—comes to heal his relationship with Victor by asking: "You don't feel the need to heal anything" (97).

In Arthur Miller's 1994 play, *Broken Glass*, the actions of Doctor Harry Hyman as an atypical healer are pivotal in forcing the two main characters to resolve their emotional and sexual conflicts. The drama focuses on the relationship between Sylvia and Phillip Gellburg, American Jews living in Brooklyn in 1938. The play's central action probes the reasons for Sylvia's sudden physical paralysis which ostensibly is caused by her hysteria about the persecution of Jews in

Germany. However, paralysis works on literal and figurative levels in the play: Sylvia's physical paralysis is symptomatic of an emotional and sexual paralysis between her and her husband, Phillip. Although Doctor Harry Hyman is engaged to treat Sylvia's paralysis, his real interest in her is not wholly professional. The play details Hyman's sexual prowess, his past history with women, including extra-marital affairs. Hyman becomes powerfully aware of Sylvia's sexual anxieties and attempts to use his sexual attraction to her to cure her paralysis; he is equally intrigued by Phillip's impotency. Ultimately, Hyman operates as a sexual healer to Sylvia and a sexual foil to Phillip, whose impotency symbolizes his own kind of paralysis.

The end of the very first scene depicts Dr. Hyman as a rather atypical healer. After Phillip leaves his office, Hyman expresses his doubts to his wife Margaret about continuing on Sylvia's case because it may not be in his professional domain as a general practitioner. Hyman admits, "I barely know my way around psychiatry. I'm not completely sure I ought to get into." But Margaret is quite aware of her husband's libido and jokes: "Why not?—She's a very beautiful woman?" Hyman matches her wryness: "Well, is that a reason to turn her away?" but admits: "Something about it fascinates me--no disease and she's paralyzed. I'd really love to give it a try...I just feel there's something about it that I understand" (27). This dialogue points to Hyman's real interest in Sylvia, an interest not wholly professional. Margaret's wry remark about Hyman's physical attraction to Sylvia underscores his sexual prowess with women. From an ethical standpoint, Hyman should refer Sylvia to another doctor, but what really "fascinates" Hyman about the case—the "something" that he "understands"—is Sylvia's sexual frustration. For Hyman will use his own sexuality to heal Sylvia's sexual paralysis with Phillip.

Act One, Scene Five—the first of two scenes when Dr. Hyman treats Sylvia alone in her bedroom—strikingly portrays how tuned-in Hyman becomes to Sylvia's sexual anxiety. Hyman blatantly expresses his sexual attraction to Sylvia by complimenting her "beautiful legs," and "strong beautiful body," even telling her "You're an attractive woman....I haven't been this moved by a woman in a very long time" (63). At the end of the scene Hyman enforces his sexual power with the unorthodox way he is treating Sylvia:

I want you to imagine that we've made love. . . . I've made
love to you. And now it's over and we are lying together. And
you begin to tell me some secret things. Things that are way
deep down in your heart. (69)

Hyman's unorthodox treatment of Sylvia is suspected by many of
the characters, and he, too, even evidences self-doubt. In the last
scene of act one, Hyman confronts Phillip about the claim that he
made love to Sylvia in her sleep the previous night. Sylvia does not
remember the act and has told Phillip he has imagined it which, of
course, is close to the truth. He has concocted the lovemaking to
cover up the fact that they have not made love in twenty years. When
Hyman offers his own doubts about the lovemaking, Phillip gets
angry at his attitude, and Hyman even asks if Sylvia has said
something to Phillip about him. At this point Phillip perceives
Hyman's odd treatment of Sylvia for he tells him he does not want
him treating her anymore saying, "Are you a doctor or what!" (83).
After Phillip leaves, Margaret senses he has trouble over the way he
has treated Sylvia. Hyman's worlds—his reputation as a doctor, his
own desire for Sylvia, his rather unorthodox treatment of her, his own
marriage—is threatened by Phillip's anger. Certainly Hyman
perceives the threat, too, when he asks Phillip, "Has she said
something about me?" (82)

Hyman's role as both sexual healer to Sylvia and foil to Phillip
reaches its climax in Act Two. Scene two begins with Hyman and
Sylvia, again alone in her room, as she recounts a violent dream she
has every night about being chased by a crowd of Germans. One man
catches her, pushes her down, gets on top of her, kisses her and then
starts to cut off her breasts. Sylvia sees the side of his face and
recognizes it as Phillip's, her acknowledgement of him as the one she
is frightened of. After this, she passionately kisses Hyman, out of
both relief and frustration, and then reveals that she and Phillip have
not slept together in over twenty years.

Hyman's role in reconciling Phillip to Sylvia and his Jewishness
also is crucial. Phillip struggles not only to find his identity as man,
but particularly as a Jewish man, which he has avoided his whole life.
However, Phillip cannot get beyond his overriding concern with his
sexual inadequacy because he blames Hyman for Sylvia's looking
down on him "like a miserable piece of shit" (131). However, Hyman
ultimately forces Phillip to look at the persecution of the Jews as what

he has been doing to his own Jewishness and what he has wrought on himself and Sylvia.

Despite Hyman's role as an atypical healer, he enables Sylvia and Phillip to heal themselves before the dramatic end of the play when Phillip collapses on his bed and Sylvia dramatically rises, stepping out of her wheelchair toward him. Hyman's sexuality acts as a catalyst for the resolution of their sexual and emotional paralysis.

Finally, critics have noted that many of Miller's plays where the law is a central focus are actually located in courts, legal chambers, tribunals, or places which are effectively transformed into places of judgment. Similarly, the same can be observed about Miller's plays where the medical profession or ethics are highlighted. Obviously, *The Last Yankee* takes place in an institution; *The Ride Down Mt. Morgan* in a hospital; and many scenes in *Broken Glass* occur in the offices of Dr. Harry Hyman. But in *Broken Glass* Sylvia Gellburg's bedroom also is transformed into an examination room, and the same can be observed about the attic room in *The Price* when Walter goes off to examine the ninety year old Solomon, who has taken ill. *Incident at Vichy* contains the analyst's room of LeDuc while off stage the professor, in a gross violation of medical ethics, examines the detainees' penises. One could argue that the stage in *After the Fall* is Quentin's analyst's couch.

Also, Jane Dominik has written about the significance of absent characters in Miller's dramatic canon (119). Included in this are the large number of absent doctors who have a major impact in the particular play's action. For example, the hysteria of the girls at the beginning of *The Crucible* is misdiagnosed by Dr. Griggs, who in the opening lines of the play, Abigail reports, "can find no medicine for it in his book," which, of course, gives way to the books of Reverend Hale, who offers quite a different examination and diagnosis. Griggs also finds that the nearly 60 year old Sarah Good is pregnant. In *Incident at Vichy*, there is the mention of the absent doctor, a Nazi collaborator, the cousin of Von Berg who had exiled Jewish doctors. LeDuc confronts Von Berg with this, which leads to his awareness. There are the absent psychiatrists in *The Archbishop's Ceiling* who prescribe feel good medication for Adrian's wife, Ruth. The absent Doctor Rockwell in *The Last Yankee* does not even realize that Patricia is not taking her medication. In *The Ride Down Mt. Morgan* the nurse refers to the doctor not wanting Lyman staying "under too long." Is he not "under" most of the play?

All of Miller's doctors—whether major, minor, or absent—confront the time-honored principle of "emotional detachment" upon which the profession is based.

Notes

[1] Thomas Adler describes "shadings" (87) in Stockmann's character and the inclusion of a politically charged speech by Peter Stockman, the town's mayor, who leads the charge against his brother.

[2] Miller's interest in psychology is well documented. See Richard I. Evans. *Psychology and Arthur Miller*. It is notable that psychology and psychologists are particularly heightened in both *Incident at Vichy* and the play which preceded it only 11 months before, *After the Fall*, in which a psychiatrist plays a significant role as an absent character, if we judge that the person whom Quentin addresses throughout the play is an analyst.

Works Cited

Adler, Thomas P. "Conscience and Community in *An Enemy of the People* and *The Crucible*." In *Cambridge Companion to Arthur Miller*. Edited by Christopher Bigsby. Cambridge: Cambridge University Press, 1997. 86-100.

Bigsby, Christopher. "Miller in the Nineties." In *Cambridge Companion to Arthur Miller*. Edited by Christopher Bigsby. Cambridge: Cambridge University Press, 1997. 168-183.

Carson, Neil. *Arthur Miller*. New York: Grove, 1982.

Centola, Steven, R. "Bad Faith and *All My Sons*." In *All My Sons, Modern Critical Interpretations*. Edited by Harold Bloom. New York: Chelsea House, 1988. 123-33.

Dominik, Jane. "A View from *Death of a Salesman*." In *"The Salesman Has a Birthday": Essays Celebrating the Fiftieth Anniversary of Arthur Miller's Death of a Salesman*. Edited by Stephen Marino. Lanham, MD: University Press of America, 2000. 109-31.

Evans, Richard I. *Psychology and Arthur Miller*. New York: E.P. Dutton, 1969.

Lowenthal, Lawrence D. "Arthur Miller's *Incident at Vichy*: A Sartrean Interpretation." *Modern Drama* 18 (1975): 29-41.

Miller, Arthur. *All My Sons*. New York: Penguin, 2000.

————. *An Enemy of the People.* New York: Penguin, 1979.

————. *Broken Glass.* New York: Penguin, 1994.

————. *Incident at Vichy.* New York: Penguin, 1985.

————. *The Price.* New York: Penguin, 1985.

————. *The Ride Down Mt. Morgan.* New York: Penguin, 1991.

Otten. Terry. *The Temptation of Innocence in the Dramas of Arthur Miller.* Missouri: University of Missouri Press, 2002.

Roth, Martin. "Sept-D'un-Coup." In *Critical Essays on Arthur Miller.* Edited by James Martine. Boston: G.K. Hall, 1979. 108-11.

Welland, Dennis. *Miller the Playwright.* London and New York: Methuen, 1979.

Miller, Marriage, and Middle America: An Uneasy Embrace

Carlos Campo

"Wedlock, as old men note, hath likened been
Unto a publick crowd or common rout,
Where those that are without would fain get in
And those that are within would fain get out."
–Poor Richard's Almanac

Leave it to Benjamin Franklin to disparage the sanctity of the American institution of marriage. Dr. Sonya Ruth Das, in her 1948 text *The American Woman in Modern Marriage*, takes a far more conservative stance when she writes that:

> Marriage leads to the foundation of the family. The modern family is a partnership between husband and wife, each of whom contributes to its development and takes responsibility for its maintenance. Their separate interests are combined and coordinated and divergent sentiments, aspirations, desires, aims and ideals adjusted for common welfare. It is the success of this partnership, coordination and co-adaptation on which depends the happiness of the modern American family. (121)

Writing eleven years later in *American Marriage: A Way of Life*, Ruth Cavan echoes Das' sentiments:

Mutual love is basic to the formation of the American family
group. In time, love grows to mutual concern for the happiness
and welfare of each member. Each is thus influenced by the
wishes of the other members; each wishes to help the others.
Since this relationship is mutual, each not only gives affection,
but also receives it in return. This mutuality gives
cohesiveness to the family. No one who is a member of a we-
group ever walks completely alone. (74)

Against the backdrop of these traditional views of marriage, enters
America's foremost playwright of the period, Arthur Miller.
Marriage figures prominently in many of Miller's plays, and it is
unquestionably a predominant theme in three of his most recent
dramas: *Broken Glass*, *The Ride Down Mount Morgan*, and *The Last
Yankee*. The view of marriage which emerges from Miller's plays is
complex, but has often been overshadowed by the overwhelming
focus on other issues, such as the father-son relationships in his
drama. With few exceptions, these marriages are fractured,
tumultuous affairs, torn by adultery, and shattered by selfishness and
bitterness. While it might be tempting to conclude that Miller sees
marriage as a restrictive and outmoded social construct, it is evident
that he believes that marriage can be a unifying agent in a world of
separateness. Speaking to Philip Gelb about his work in 1958, Miller
says that, "I think that the drama, at least mine, is not so much an
attack as an exposition, so to speak, of the want of value, and you can
only do this if the audience is constantly trying to supply what is
missing" (35). If stable, healthy marriages are often "missing" in
Miller's work, it is probably more of an attempt to expose a social
weakness rather than propound a personal view. A close analysis of
marriage in Miller's drama seems to suggest not a rejection, but an
underlying embrace, however uneasy, of the Middle American ideal
of marriage.

The *American Heritage Dictionary* defines Middle America as
"that part of the U.S. middle class thought of as being average in
income and education and moderately conservative in values and
attitudes." Miller establishes his connection to Middle America in his
autobiography *Timebends*. The phrase occurs twice in the work, both
times referring to his visit to Ohio to wed his first wife, Mary
Slattery. He refers to Mary's Aunt Helen as one who "emitted the
power of the distracted, the air of the Middle American searcher"
(87). He later recounts a visit with Mary's extended family, focusing

on her grandmother, who took a liking to Miller and commented that she liked him "being so tall." As Mary sits down beside her grandmother and clasps her hand, the old gal pats Miller's knee and he proclaims, "An immense feeling of safety crept over me as we sat there in the middle of America" (81).

If any Miller drama captures the spirit of Middle America, the leading candidate would seem to be *All My Sons*. The play opens with a description of the back yard of a home on the "*outskirts of an American town*" (201). The dialogue begins with a discussion of American icons: tobacco, the weather, the newspaper. Miller has often commented that he was trying to capture the tone and atmosphere of Slattery's Ohio in this play. One of the most interesting lines regarding marriage in *All My Sons* is spoken by neighbor Dr. Jim Bayliss who is comforting Kate about Chris's sudden departure and says that he once left his wife for two months to study a certain disease, but then "she came, and she cried. And I went back home with her. And now I live in the usual darkness; I can't find myself; it's even hard sometimes to remember the kind of man I wanted to be. I'm a good husband; Chris is a good son—he'll come back" (277). Bayliss's lines run counter to the middle American sentiments regarding marriage in 1947, and certainly undercut Chris and Ann's hope that their marriage will erase the Kellers' dark past as it initiates their blessed future together.

While the play features three married couples and a fourth on the way, the drama truly centers on Chris and Joe Keller, culminating in Joe's epiphany-turned-title. In *Timebends*, Miller comments on an Israeli version of the play which focused on Kate Keller, writing that she was emphasized in the original production, but "bypassed in favor of the father-son conflict" (135). Miller claims that Kate's knowledge of Joe's crime, "so obdurately and menacingly suppressed, can be interpreted. . .primarily, as her wish to take vengeance on her culpable husband by driving him psychically to his knees and ultimately to suicide" (135-36). The play would suggest that Kate's dark wish is suppressed so completely it is nearly non-existent. When Joe sits "*slumped in his chair*" in the agony of his final despair and asks "What am I gonna do Kate," she cries out: "Joe, Joe, please...you'll be all right, nothing is going to happen. . ." (280). She later tries to keep Joe from the letter that leads to his final, desperate act with "Go to the street, Joe, go to the street! Don't Chris. . .Don't tell him. . ." (286). These passages seem to characterize Kate as Miller does in the play, a "*woman with an overwhelming capacity for love*" (215), not as a wife with a subliminized, dark intent. Yet, this duality strikes at the heart of the view of marriage in Miller's work. Writing about his marriage to Mary Slattery in *Timebends*, he comments that he was "trying to repair a marriage that mutual intolerance was slowly destroying" (146). He points out that analysis simply confirmed what he already knew:

> My father appeared as a deanimated and forbidding avenger who I knew was and was not my actual father. My mother was and was not the woman who was tempting me sensually to capture her from my father, and was culpable of both disloyalty to him and, as herself, perfectly innocent. Until I began to write plays my frustration with this doubleness of reality was terrible, but once I could impersonate all conflicts on a third plane, the plane of art, I was able to enjoy my power—even if a twinge of shame continued to accompany the plays into the world. (146)

This artistic vision—what Miller calls a "doubleness"—has engendered Kate Keller as lover and destroyer, Linda Loman as crippling enabler and dutiful wife, Quentin as conniving murderer and blessed savior, Harry Hyman as a detached physician and competing lover, Lyman Felt as a sensual egoist and provident husband, and Leroy Hamilton as a confident partner and a defeated man. All of these are terribly reductive and hence limited, yet a strand of truth remains in them.

What is the "twinge of shame" that Miller says accompany his plays into the world? Did Miller feel the sense of personal loss that Bayliss refers to? In *Timebends*, he relates how, only a week after his marriage to Mary Grace Slattery (he refers to her as such despite the fact that she is Mary Grace Miller), he launches out on a "solo honeymoon," to satisfy his "lust for experience" (70) and research the background for a play. Mary is there to see him off, and Miller writes that "This early parting, like our marriage—and perhaps most marriages in our time—was a refusal to surrender the infinitude of options that we at least imagined we had. I would not yet have believed that our characters leave us far fewer choices than we like to concede" (70).

Miller revisits marriage in his next play, *Death of a Salesman*, and places the taboo of adultery at the core of the drama's central conflict. Cavan's text, written ten years after *Salesman*'s opening, reveals the

Middle American view of adultery. In a section entitled "Common Symptoms of Trouble within the Marriage," she lists "Feeling that one's personal needs are not being met in the marriage; in extreme cases finding 'consolation' outside of marriage with the 'other woman'—or man" (353). Of course, Willy and Linda's is not an "extreme case" any more than Nora and Torvald Helmer's was some sixty years previously, but Miller, like Ibsen, hopes to reflect a morality that mirrors his society more effectively than other popular dramas. Beyond Miller's iconoclastic use of adultery, *Salesman* may be the only Miller play where marriage has been rather thoroughly discussed, and a review here would be superfluous. It is important to note, however; that Linda shares some crucial similarities with her prototype, Kate Keller. She possesses Kate's remarkable capacity to love a terribly flawed man, and her struggle to save Willy from his inexorable fate parallels Kate's futility to rescue Joe.

Over the next decade, marital strife, adultery, and taboo topics resurface in Miller's most celebrated dramas of the period, *The Crucible* and *A View From the Bridge*. Miller's personal life is in shambles; in the six-year period from 1956-62, he divorces Mary Slattery, marries Marilyn Monroe, divorces Monroe, marries Inge Morath and endures Monroe's death. Once again, Miller turns to his "third plane" of art to merge his suffering with his version of Camus' *The Fall*, and revisits marriage in an unprecedented way. Though Miller hoped to go beyond what he saw as the theme of Camus' novel, "the trouble with women," his play inevitably revolves around Quentin's relationship with Louise, Maggie and Holga.

In *After the Fall*, Miller gives us Quentin, the deeply flawed egoist, who is determined to understand his failed relationships, his "two divorces in his safe deposit box" (3). Unlike Miller husbands of the past, Quentin has no easy answers, only a pervasive sense of hope that he is determined to either destroy or foster. In Quentin, we do not hear the simplistic rationales of "I was terribly lonely" or "It needs a cold wife to prompt lechery." Instead, Quentin does not know what people are to one another any longer, cannot give advice, lay blame, but only stare out into the darkness at the faceless Listener in hopes that he can find a part of himself that is able to move forward through the ashes of his past.

Quentin is stunned that after all he has lived through, he still is like a boy, open to the world, a sentiment reflected in his comments to Louise: "Yes. She has legs, breasts, mouth, eyes. . .how beautiful! A woman of my own! What a miracle! In my own house! *He bends and kisses Louise who looks up at him surprised, perplexed"* (52). Louise's perplexity undoubtedly derives from the fact that Quentin sounds like an eight-year old who just discovered a Tonka truck under his bed, with tires and lights that really flash! Yet there is a sincerity to Quentin's misguided boyish euphoria regarding his spouse that contrasts Louise's sterile, often dour responses. Quentin cannot accept Louise's view that he must view her as a separate person. He says, "When you've finally become a separate person, what the hell is there" (42)? Iska Alter rightly comments that Quentin is fearful of "his wife's efforts to establish an independent, feminine self" (147). Quentin would likely admit this fear, as throughout the drama he is fighting separateness as the most destructive force in humanity—one of Miller's transcendent themes. Moreover, Quentin's aversion to separateness may also be linked to the fundamental biblical principle of the man and woman cleaving to one another as they "become one flesh," a testament against separateness, inherent in the Middle American view of marriage. Quentin refuses to let any man put asunder his view that "underneath we're all profoundly friends."

Quentin cannot simply dismiss Louise by flinging his spiteful "Bitch!" toward her exit. They struggle together for three years after their dramatized blow-up, hoping for something to "save" them. Quentin confesses that they would hold hands and "laugh it all back to—her dear, honest face looking up at mine. . .back to some everlasting smile that saves. That's maybe why I came; I think I still believe it. I can't believe this world; all this hatred isn't real to me" (61). It is Quentin's memory of Louise's saving smile—despite their conflicts—that initiates his search, and hence the entire drama. As the force that inspires the play, her role is more central than many critics concede. Alter minimizes Louise's importance as she sees the play as "Quentin's responses to the demanding complexity of feminine force as enacted by the three women who have made, shattered, and recorded his existence: Mother, Maggie and Holga" (141). Alter further asserts that Louise is given a "collateral role as a wife who practices the treachery of betrayal" (144). Yet, what exactly is Louise's betrayal? Surely it is not the fact that she turned her back on Quentin in bed or forced him to sleep on the couch and lie to his daughter in the morning about having a cold. There is no woman from Boston here, no bewitching teen, just a failure of the will. Quentin honestly admits that Louise is simply a "stranger he had never gotten to know." When the lawyer in Quentin searches for grounds for this divorce, he will be forced to examine the truth of Louise's claim for what their breakup is "all about": "You don't want me." Quentin can only respond, "God! Can that be true" (57) seemingly aware that it indeed is—despite the haunting recollection of her everlasting, saving smile.

Quentin's ambivalence regarding his divorce seems to mirror Miller's doubts regarding his divorce of Mary Slattery. When Mel Gussow commented to Miller in 1987 that Quentin's lines are closest to Miller in an emotional if not autobiographical way, Miller responded with: "I would say that's valid. It's the one in which I was most directly trying to figure out my relationship to all kinds of moral problems that I thought everyone else faced, as well as myself. The death of love—and the rest of it. And it's the most personal statement I've ever made" (152). In a 2001 interview with Gussow, Miller was asked if he had ever faced calamity, and responded: "Eight or ten times! I came to the edge of life a number of times, once with the House Un-American Activities Committee. Then with my divorce. I was married seventeen years. That was a big blow, that I would come to that" (25). In *Timebends*, Miller writes extensively about his feelings at that time. In one passage he admits, "I no longer knew what I wanted—certainly not the end of my marriage, but the thought of putting Marilyn out of my life was unbearable" (356). In another, he claims:

> I deeply wanted to be one, not divided, to speak with the same voice in private and publicly. I did not see why marriage and family necessarily imposed strategies of subtle self-censorship, not so subtle subterfuge, and implicit betrayal. But I lacked the courage to declare in so many words that I was no longer speciously whole, as I had been, and that the future for me was no longer known. I retreated into silence, uncertain of what I might say and what was prohibited, for I had already passed beyond conventions, beyond a commonsensical awareness of what one's partner should or could be called upon to bear. (327)

He later declares:

> I was so at odds with myself, with Mary, and with the undeniable inner pressure to break out of what had come to seem an emptied, self-denying carapace. I wanted to stop

turning away from the power that my work had won for me, and to engorge experience forbidden in a life of disciplined ambition, at the same time dreading the consequences—less to myself, perhaps, than to those I loved. . .Cautiously at first, or so I fatuously thought, I let the mystery and blessing of womankind break like waves over my head once or twice, enough to shatter for me the last belief that social arrangements, including marriage, had something to do with inevitability. (312)

While the preceding quote would seem to suggest that Miller came to see marriage as a confining, empty dyad, at a much later point in his autobiography, he suggests otherwise:

I had moved into the unknown, physically as well as spiritually, and the color of the unknown is darkness until it opens into the light.

    But there were only glimmers so far. Divorce, I suppose, is to some degree an optimistic reaching for authenticity, a rebellion against waste. But we are mostly what we were, and the turtle stretching toward delicious buds on high does not lighten his carapace by his resolve. I had to wonder sometimes if I had managed to evade rather than to declare the reality of myself. (378)

Miller struggled with the feeling that his divorce was an evasion, even as his love for Marilyn grew. In *Timebends*, he tells of a stunning epiphany in the Nevada desert that brought him clarity—at least for the moment:

I felt healed, as though I had crossed over a division within me and onto a plane of peace where the parts of myself had joined. I loved her as though I had loved her all my life; her pain was mine. . . . The anguish of the past year, the guilty parting with children and the wrenching up of roots, seemed now the necessary price for what might be truly waiting ahead, a creative life with undivided soul. . . . To be one thing, sexuality and mind, appetite and justice, one. . . . With all her concealed pain, she was. . .the astonishing signal of liberation and its joys. Out of the muck, the flower. And soon, an amazing life... (381)

But Miller's fancy did not cheat so well as she was famed to do. On the 42nd day of his Nevada residency, he endured the courthouse routine of a Reno divorce, packed his bags, and "stared out at the bony hills that I was sure I would never see again and found a kind of remorse in myself for the lost silence I had come to depend on each morning when I woke. . .Noise awaited me—was it all a mistake? I wiped out the thought, condemning my own vice of self-sufficiency" (388).

What followed with Marilyn was months of agony that led Miller to "imagine miracles" where he would tell her that God loved her and she would believe it. He wished they both had their faith intact, but the realization came that he "had no saving mystery to offer her. . .I had lost my faith in a lasting cure coming from me, and I wondered if indeed it could come from any human agency at all" (483). Miller now found himself at the end of Camus' *The Fall*, as the judge-penitent transformed into a Quentin that saw the girl, Maggie, jump off the bridge, and in the terrifying egoism of his own name, he leaps in to save her. Quentin's actions metaphorically parallel the marital act of moving from singleness—separateness, if you will—seen in Clamence's amoral safety of the apathy of non-action, to leaping off that bridge into marriage, where two learn to swim as one or drown in the imperious waters of conflict and bitterness. Miller makes the connection complete as he describes Maggie's suicide in terms that recall the agony of a drowning victim: *"Now deep, strange breathing. He quickly goes to her, throws her onto her stomach for artificial respiration"* (112).

Of course, Miller's play does not end there any more than Miller's life ended with Marilyn's death. Quentin is able to reach through the failed relationships of his past to Holga, who seems to hold out the promise a fulfilling relationship of equality which reinforces Miller's embrace—however tenuous—of the ideal American marriage. Many saw Miller's marriage to Inge Morath as his personal reflection of Quentin's restorative connection. Miller writes that although he often felt that he "should never form another commitment again" because "we are all too much like music," with Inge he came to know that "No partner ought to be asked to contribute to silence. In this year of knowing one another, the simplest of ideas—that I needed help in order to live—became not only obvious but honorable and even a kind of strength" (502).

Some thirty years later, in this renewed sense of the power of marriage, Miller returns to marriage as a primary subject of three plays he will complete in the three years, all, like *After the Fall*, dedicated to Inge Morath: *Broken Glass*, *The Ride Down Mount Morgan*, and *The Last Yankee*. While each of these plays reinforces the power of marriage to some degree, they also employ dark images of physical and mental illness. *Broken Glass* recounts the story of Sylvia Gellburg, who nine days before the start of the play, loses feeling in her legs after seeing the events of Kristallnacht in the newspaper. Her husband Phillip, desperate for any help, seeks out a local "wunderdoctor" for help. Into the Gellburg's lives rides Hymen, the god of marriage, thinly disguised as Dr. Harry Hyman, whose horse and riding crop have supplanted Hymen's wings and bridal torch. Dr. Hyman quickly realizes that just as when Aphrodite cursed the isle of Lemnos, "chill neglect" has come "o'er the lawful couch" of the Gellburg's wedding bed, and they have not had sex in some twenty years. The Gellburg's separation is the result of a combination of complex factors, including Phillip's abusive nature, his impotence, and his idealization of his wife. Dr. Hyman tries to breathe life into Sylvia's shriveled heart by telling her that the "depth of her flesh must be wonderful" and that he hasn't "been this moved by a woman in a very long time" (70), expressions of physical intimacy that surely have not been expressed to Sylvia for some time. When Hyman admits that he's "out of his depth" and can't help her, Sylvia says that only he can save her. She grasps his hands, kisses him, and cries out, "Help me. Please" (113)! Sylvia's pleas mirror Kassandra's desperate entreaties to the god in Euripides' *Trojan Women*: "Master of my maiden flesh, take me! Heaven's blessing falls on me and falls on you. Hear my cry of worship, Hymen, God of hot desire! Dancers, come! Loose your leaping feet, wild with wine of ecstasy!" (310) Dr. Hyman encourages Sylvia to loose her feet as well when he says "You should be dancing, you should be stretching in the sun" (70).

Phillip will also bow before the god of marriage in desperate supplication late in the play: *"his body quakes; crying out:* Hyman...Help me! *Ashamed of his outburst, he covers his face"* (144). He fears that Hyman's emotional attachment to his wife will lead him to pose as a surrogate lover who offers sexual healing. In the play's climactic scene, Phillip, Sylvia and Hyman are together at Phillip's bedside where he is trying to recover from a recent collapse. Phillip erupts with, "Hyman! I only ask one thing—don't do it in this house" (155). He then begs Sylvia to stop her charade and stand up. He tries to draw her up by the arm when Hyman calls out—not without irony—"You must get back in bed!" Phillip collapses to the floor; Hyman rushes to help him but cannot reach the life-giving oxygen while he pumps Phillip's chest with one hand. Miraculously, Sylvia gets to her feet, and hands Hyman the oxygen mask, who places it on Phillip's face. Then, embodying both the god of marriage and Cupid, Hyman plunges a needle into Phillip's chest, and as his soul is released by the arrow's shaft, Sylvia, with arms raised, can only utter her loving "incantation": "Oh Phillip. Oh Phillip. Oh Phillip..." She gives thanks to Hyman, as she confirms that her feeling "came back," to which Hyman can only respond, "My God" (156-58)! At the close of the play, Hyman's blessing is conferred, and a "straight and fine" Sylvia's focus has returned to her husband, as she kisses his hand and continues to call out to him, "Please! Please ...please, Phillip, look at me..." (161).

In *The Ride Down Mount Morgan*, Miller unleashes Lyman Felt, an anthropomorphized libido who rationalizes his bigamy in a play that—at face value—would seem to undermine traditional views of marriage. Lyman has the remarkable vitality of Milton's Satan and Browning's Bishop from St. Praxed's Church, but also shares their moral vacuity. With all his blustering, at the close of the play, he is lonely and afraid, begging Nurse Logan to stay with him. He asks her to recount an ice-fishing trip she shared with her family, where they passed the time by talking about their new shoes. Lyman is so touched by the simple beauty of that moment—and its brief, but powerful representation of a Middle American family—that he weeps, wondering at "What a miracle everything is" (141)! Nurse Logan and Lyman's lawyer, a Quaker named Tom Wilson who proudly declares that he has never cheated on his wife, stand in stark contrast to Lyman and his ludicrous attempts to defend his infamy. Though clearly idealized to a point, they quietly remind the audience of the dignity found in living morally. June Schlueter writes that *The Ride Down Mount Morgan* has been read as "a questioning of monogamy as the prevailing marital structure of the Western world" (143), yet she concludes that the play's elusiveness leads to "an unfinished portrait of a life needing verification but trapped within the shifting boundaries and orthodox marital morality of Miller's play" (149).

The more conservative elements in *The Ride Down Mount Morgan* seem to presage Miller's *The Last Yankee*, a drama which celebrates the American ideal of marriage as a hedge against the disconnected isolation so common in Miller's works. *The Last Yankee* is Leroy Hamilton, the quintessential American, descended from Alexander

Hamilton, but devoid of the latter's elitism. He is the devoted bread-
winning father of seven. He uses Stanley tools, chooses the American
banjo over the Spanish guitar, and, most importantly, he is a
dedicated husband to his suffering wife, Patricia. It is Patricia's third
visit to a state mental hospital; it is her third week without
medication; and both the Hamiltons are hoping that the uniquely
American phrase of "third time's the charm" applies to them.[1]

When we meet Patricia in Scene Two, she is asking another patient,
Karen Frick, "Why are we doing this? Come, let's talk, I hate these
games" (21), referring to a Ping-Pong game they've been playing.
Patricia's opening lines may metaphorically relate to her marriage, as
something has changed in her feelings toward Leroy, and she is ready
to speak with him about going home—tired of the back and forth
bickering and the game-playing represented in the Ping-Pong image.
Patricia tells Karen that she has had a revelation: "It came to me like
a visitation two weeks ago, I-must-not-blame-Leroy-anymore. And
it's amazing, I lost all desire for medication, I could feel it leaving me
like a. . .like a ghost" (26). Patricia has been blaming Leroy for not
fulfilling her expectations, which are centered on one of Miller's
favorite topics: money. She grates that Leroy has well-to-do relatives
but refuses to ask for help, that while men with half his ability have
big expensive cars, his car's rear end has collapsed for the second
Easter Sunday in a row; that she must suffer the ignominy of riding
around in a nine-year-old Chevrolet, that he spends money on banjo
lessons, is talking about donating his valuable tool collection to a
museum, and that he never seems to charge what he's worth for his
carpentry. We also learn that Patricia's two over-achieving brothers
wound up committing suicide because of disappointment. She
explains, "We were all brought up expecting to be wonderful, and
. . .just wasn't" (33). Now Patricia must overcome her own
disappointment or face her brothers' fate.

Patricia acknowledges how Leroy has supported her, saying that
she's even ashamed when she thinks of him "hanging in there all
these years" (26). She seems surprised to learn that he has never
cheated on her, and when she wants to know why not, he poignantly
replies: "I'd remember you happy and loving—that's what's kept me
. . .When you're positive about life there's just nobody like you.
Nobody. Not in life, not in the movies, Not on TV" (45). Yet, Leroy's
steadfastness is simply not enough. Patricia despairs that her life will
never really change, and she'll never feel that it's a wonderful as she
imagines that it should be. Leroy admits that "this is pretty much it,"

although to him "it's already wonderful—I mean the kids, and there are some clear New England mornings when you want to drink the air and the sunshine" (46).

The wonderful comes to Patricia when she sees the interaction between Karen and her husband John Frick. They are the privileged, the very rich who Patricia says have no right to be depressed. They have all the things—those wondrous objects—that Patricia longs for, including a new car and pockets full of money. But as Patricia talks to John, she realizes how much they lack. Karen likes to tap dance, but John admits that he "never thought about it one way or another" (51). Patricia asks John to stop criticizing her, and instead, to support her. John's feelings are put to the test when Karen enters, dressed in satin shorts, a tailcoat, a high hat, tap shoes, and walking stick, and strikes a theatrical pose for good measure. At the height of her vulnerability, one that every performer knows, she is desperate for some reinforcement from her spouse. John tries to join in at first, even "unhappily" singing a few bars of Swanee River as Karen taps away, before he explodes in anger and leaves in embarrassment. Patricia and Leroy try to encourage Karen to continue, but after a few feeble steps, she walks out in "unrelieved sadness" (56).

At this moment, Patricia and Leroy move through a wordless vignette that reflects the profound change in Patricia. She reaches out and touches his face with "muted gratitude," then goes and packs her things to leave. When she comes out of the room he laughs, on the verge of weeping, to ask the terrifying question, "Ready?" She can only muster, "Leroy. . .I can't believe it. . .I've had nothing" (56). Patricia now refers to more than just her medication; she has come to realize that she's had "nothing," as she rejects the materialism that has paralyzed her in the past. She now knows that she's had a great "something," a husband who truly loves her in spite of her uncertainty and vulnerability, a family that is going to be happy to have her home. After witnessing Karen's pain, Patricia has followed Leroy's advice and now loves the world as she sees that what is most wonderful is what we often take for granted, but—for Patricia—no more: she completes the moment of insight with "Thank you," as she *draws him to her and kisses him*"(57). One can almost hear Quentin's voice calling out to the Hamiltons: "No, it's not certainty. I don't feel that. But it does seem feasible...not to be afraid" (114).

With *The Last Yankee* Arthur Miller solidifies his pervasive view that marriage, like friendship, is a way for a man to transform an often embittered, hostile world into a home. Though his feelings are not absolute, it is clear that Miller did not allow the sometimes-dark events in his life destroy his belief in the ideal of marriage in America. Twenty-five years after the events that might have produced an insular bitterness in a lesser man, Miller is able to write, "Maybe Ibsen had been wrong: he is not strongest who is most alone, he is just lonelier" (502).

Notes

[1] For a fuller discussion of the number three in American culture, refer to Professor Allen Dundes' book, *Every Man his Way*, Berkeley: Berkeley University Press, 1968.

Works Cited

Alter, Iska. "Betrayal and Blessedness: Explorations of Feminine Power in *The Crucible*, *A View from the Bridge*, and *After the Fall.*" In *Modern Critical Interpretations: The Crucible*. Edited by Harold Bloom. Philadelphia: Chelsea House Publishers, 1999. 108-20.

Cavan, Ruth. *American Marriage: A Way of Life*. New York: Thomas Y. Crowell, 1959.

Das, Sonya Ruth. *The American Woman in Modern Marriage*. New York: The Philosophical Library, 1948.

Euripides. *Trojan Women. Hecuba; The Trojan Women; Andromache/Euripides; translated with explanatory notes by James Morwood; with introduction by Edith Hall.* New York: Oxford University Press, 2000. 38-76.

Gelb, Philip. "Morality and Modern Drama." *Conversations with Arthur Miller.* Jackson: University of Mississippi Press, 1987. 35-51.

Gussow, Mel. *Conversations with Miller*. New York: Applause Theatre and Cinema Books, 2002.

Miller, Arthur. *All My Sons*. In *Famous American Plays of the 1940s.* New York: Laurel Press, 1960. 199-290.

———. *After the Fall*. New York: Viking, 1964.

———. *Broken Glass*, New York: Penguin Plays, 1994.

———. *The Last Yankee*. In *The Last Yankee with a New Essay About Theatre Language and Broken Glass*. New York: Fireside Theatre, 1994.

————. *The Ride Down Mount Morgan*. New York: Penguin Plays, 1992.

Schleuter, June. "Scripting the Closing Scene: Arthur Miller's *The Ride Down Mount Morgan*." In *The Achievement of Arthur Miller: New Essays*. Edited by Steven R. Centola. Dallas: Contemporary Research Press, 1995. 143-49.

Arthur Miller and the Language of Middle America

George P. Castellitto

Arthur Miller's plays invariably and consistently depict characters moving, shifting, and repositioning themselves in particularly American landscapes. As those characters involve themselves in the conflicts that comprise the various plays and as their dialogue progresses, the reader and the viewer/listener of Miller's drama is able to perceive the dialects and the idioms of the American psyche. Several of Miller's plays communicate the distinct idioms of urban and cosmopolitan America, but underlying and underpinning those urban expressions are the psychological and sociological tenets of Middle America resonating and resounding throughout and within the various speeches of the characters. In the assertions, dreams, queries, and regretful reminiscences of Willy Loman, John Proctor, Eddie Carbone, and Victor Franz lie the yearning for a wider expanse and the possibility of a more socially and psychologically gratifying frontier securely distant from the diminishing and crippling urban construct in which they find themselves. The language of each of the characters resonates between two poles—the urban walls that confine them and the remote but potential manifest destiny that beckons them to a forgotten, barely perceivable heartland and its accouterments. Both Willy Loman and John Proctor discern release and possibility of self-determination in the distant land that beckons them, that offers them movement away from the urban constructs that detain them (Brooklyn and Salem) and immersion into the barely touchable, almost insubstantial land. Ruby Cohn intimates that Willy's reveries about nature ("The trees are so thick, and the sun is warm") and

Proctor's reverence for lilacs ("Massachusetts is a beauty in the spring!") transforms the dialogue from urban colloquial to a more mannered, rural rhetoric (79). In *Death of a Salesman* as well as in *The Crucible, The Price,* and *A View from the Bridge,* a noticeable conflict arises between urban "machine" and rural "garden"; the machine persists as the "source of all industry and a competitive economic system" while the garden embodies the sense of "peace and the good life" (Pradhan 69) so characteristic of Middle America.

As the plays portray the variables so typical of urban existence, the inhabitants of that urban construct express themselves in dialogical representations that are superficially, singularly metropolitan, but implied and submerged beneath those urban expressions are echoes of the American heartland, vowels and syllables that resonate from Middle American roots in both discernibly concrete and metaphorical respects. Mikhail Bakhtin's assertions about heteroglossia, the presence of a multitude of voices in character dialogue, apply significantly if the listener/perceiver of the words of Willy, Proctor, Eddie, and Victor is to comprehend the several layers that operate dialogically in those characters' words. The heteroglossaic nature of those utterances ranges beyond the obvious presence of sublimated psyche, sociological influence, and metaphysical shadows; another "voice" that rears its head, sometimes implicitly and sometimes stridently, is that of Middle America, the geographical and cultural expanse beyond Brooklyn, Manhattan, and Salem. Discussing the concept of heteroglossia from a different perspective than that of Bakhtin, Jacques Derrida explains the roles of the representer (the speaker or actor) and the represented (the character being portrayed) and how that relationship as it progresses on the page and stage necessarily summons in both language and metaphor a more prominent sociological construct that reverberates within and around the dialogue (Derrida 305). That "other" social structure that emerges from the words is that of Middle America, sometimes barely visible, always alluring and beckoning, and frequently both the source and the end of the character's machinations.

In his book *Tragedy and Fear: Why Modern Tragic Drama Fails,* John von Szeliski discusses the tonic chord and poetic structure of the speeches of various Miller characters (143); often, the poetic composition of the language of the characters depicts a tension between confinement (frequently denoted by references to the city) and possible freedom (the distant, almost untouchable country). For example, when John Proctor decides to grasp his name and thus chooses death, he is asserting that all that could possibly save his life, the act of self-denial that would discount his sense of self, is merely a re-immersion into the narrow and constricting values of Salem; his rejection of those principles brings to him an enlightenment (von Szeliski 181), a true embracing of Middle American values in the final grasping of his name. Therefore, in essence, that embracing of his name, the "honor" and goodness" mentioned in the play's final lines, is transformed into the language of Middle America, a dialect that rejects the restrictive hypocrisy of Salem and adopts a philosophy of freedom and expansiveness. The same tension between urban and rural, between the colloquialisms of the streets and the poetic diction of the Middle American landscape and horizon occurs in *Death of a Salesman* where past and present, middle America and urban America, collapse into each other to portray not only Willy's disintegrating mind (Bigsby, *Twentieth Century American Drama* 183) but also the connection between the aspects and expressions of urban and Middle America. C. W. E. Bigsby discusses this bond between urban present and Middle American past in *Salesman*:

> Willy Loman's life is rooted in America's past. His earliest memory was of sitting under a wagon in South Dakota. His father had made and sold flutes as they traveled through what was still, just, frontier territory. And this remains the world of his aspirations...rather than a job that sends him wandering through New England cities.... (*Twentieth Century AD* 184)

Thus, many of Miller's characters employ language that derives from a land that distantly beckons them and that has escaped them. While the language of Eddie Carbone and Willy Loman often seemingly and superficially operates as the language of pathological denial, still a yearning for a more peaceful and self-determining landscape reverberates within their syllables. Penelope Curtis points out that the language of John Proctor and of the Salem community in general derives from a land that is potentially the landscape of Middle America:

> The two crucial factors in their lives were the land and their religion. So powerfully did these unite them that [Miller] was able to give his characters an expressive, wide-ranging idiom that draws continuously on both sources. Their speech has the saltiness, the physicality, of a life lived close to the soil... (68)

The soil, the expanse of land and frontier that is essentially non-urban America, consistently emerges in the syllables that Miller's characters utter. In *Modern American Drama*, Bigsby discusses how those characters are seeking an alternate world and yearning for a "relationship between the self and an environment undamaged by modernity "(70). In his comparison of Eddie Carbone to Melville's Ahab and Fitzgerald's Gatsby, Bigsby emphasizes Eddie's sense of a single vision (*Modern American Drama* 96), but, more significantly, Miller's characters, like Ahab and Gatsby, are aware of a distant metaphysical construct that eludes them. That construct is the landscape of Middle America, and their language, though ostensibly rooted in urban colloquialisms and street-oriented modernities, displays their awareness of that lost and distant Middle America. In Bakhtinian terms, the dialogue of the characters operates in a heteroglossaic manner where the actual words resonate as urban expressions but the psychological and sociological foundations of those utterances are Middle America and its potential frontier. Such a divergence between the actuality of the dialogue and its Middle American potentiality creates a sense of bifurcation; in *The Price*, for example, Walter and Victor represent two halves of an America displaced by the crash of 1929, and the play's language demonstrates this bifurcation and divergence between the urban reality and the Middle American potentiality.

In *Echoes Down the Corridor*, Miller describes the character of Willy Loman as "something that has never existed before, a salesman with his feet on the subway stairs and his head in the stars" (272). In the Loman language, an element more expansive than is initially evident continuously emerges, not simply in the platitudes and truisms that Willy imposes on his sons but also in the simple act of using his flashlight to read aloud on the seed packages the names of the vegetables (carrots, beets, lettuce) in Act Two. Significantly, Ben is present in this scene at the end of Act Two as Willy is planting, lamenting how the neighborhood is "boxed in," because Ben consistently represents for Willy that lost sense of American expansiveness, a frontier and perspective that even Biff seeks in his travels "on the train, in the mountains, in the valleys" (*Salesman* 129). The division between reality and possibility almost dissolves in the actual language as Willy begins to read and recite the names of the vegetables on the seed packages; his recitation separates him momentarily from his urban environment and repositions him in an Edenic, rural plot of land reminiscent of Middle America where the tenements may be ignored and the soil becomes once again productive. Thus, the actual recitation of the words become an indirect echo and refrain of the language of Middle America and its sprawling, verdant pastures, much like the sound of the flute that haunts Willy's consciousness. In his discussion of *Waiting for Godot* as a play that employs "language shorn of metaphor, simile, everything but its instructions, so that the listener may hear the theme like a nail drawn across a pane of glass," Miller contrasts Beckett's style to his own by explaining that his own tendency was "to find speech that springs naturally out of the characters and their backgrounds" (*Echoes* 311). Miller comments on how actors note that his dialogue is particularly difficult to memorize because that dialogue is indeed a type of representational, Bakhtinian, heteroglossaic discourse that places the speaker in the present both physically and psychologically but also simultaneously portrays that speaker reflecting a distant, wider, untouchable yet desirable expanse. Miller is consistently concerned with, as he expresses in *Echoes*, "the flight of the arrow. . .toward the castle of reality rather than the wayward air" (312); however, that reality is multi-faceted, encompassing not only the discernible words of the characters but also the constructs that both created those characters and that now lie detached from their psyches and experiences. The language of Middle America is continuously present in the speeches of Miller's characters in the detached but nevertheless prominent construct that always lies as the root, the possibility, or the outcome of the character's behavior.

In "The American Theater" in *Theater Essays*, Miller describes his experience of viewing Lee Cobb portraying Willy Loman:

> And the theater vanished. The stage vanished. The chill of an age-old recognition shuddered my spine; a voice was sounding in the dimly lit air up front, a created spirit, an incarnation, a Godlike creation was taking place; a new human being was being formed before all our eyes. . .; a man was transcending the limits of his body and his own history. (49)

That voice of the man in transcendence is more than that of a skilled actor (Cobb, Hoffman, Dennehy) speaking the psyche of the essential America; that voice develops as the transition and connection between urban and Middle America, a linguistic vista of utterances that roots the character in concrete but demonstrates the character's Middle American derivations. In "The Family in Modern Drama,"

Miller explains how he arranges dialogue in his plays to reflect the essentials of the speech patterns of the American family; his distinction between the employment of prose to denote the particulars of the private life and the application of verse to reflect the elements of public life (*Theater Essays* 76) applies aptly to the concept that beneath the seeming ordinariness of the urban speech patterns of the characters lies the unconscious and implied potentiality of rural, Middle America and the poetic nuances that Middle American speech patterns often embrace. Miller further discusses this heteroglossaic-like employment of language in his drama in his "Introduction to the *Collected Plays*":

> A drama, like a history, which stops at the point of conditioning, is not reflecting reality. What is wanted, therefore, is not a poetry of escape from process and determinism. . . . A new poem will appear because a new balance has been struck which embraces both determinism and the paradox of will. If there is one unseen goal toward which every play in this book strives, it is that very discovery and proof—that we are made and yet are more than what made us. (*Theater Essays* 170)

What Miller asserts here applies to his works in several arenas and modes, but, in the context of the scope of this paper, his contention about the connection between the fundamental presence of each character and the potential that reverberates in each character's words sustains the concept that, often in Miller's plays, beneath and beyond the inescapable reality of the urban lies the distant but still audible echoes of rural, Middle America. In Act One of *The Price*, Victor recollects in his conversation with Solomon how the years have slipped past in such a fleeting and ephemeral manner; Victor has chosen certain values, and though his language is that of a man burdened by years of labor in the urban "rat race" that he despises (47), nevertheless beneath his words resonate staunch values that remind the reader of ideals often associated with Middle America— loyalty to family, constancy in the face of adversity, respect for parents. Terry Otten discusses Victor's realignment with the family values that Walter abandons, and though Victor's acknowledgment of his life's inescapable options is an existential victory (156), nonetheless Victor's epiphany occurs in his transcendence of the urban jungle that has both formed and weakened him and in his embracing and reaffirmation of values frequently associated with Middle America. Just as Victor is wedged between the existential and the transcendent, Eddie Carbone, much like Willy Loman and John Proctor, is trapped between two constructs—the confines of the city and the view from the bridge to a potential America beckoning in its innocence and with its promising, verdant pastures. Though Eddie's incestuous desire becomes one of the factors that ultimately destroys him, nevertheless Eddie yearns for the facets of civilization and its inherent values; as Steven Centola explains, *A View* reflects the Freudian dialectic between order and chaos ("Compromise and Bad Faith"), an order that imparts the distant promise of a vanished Middle America whose syllables still reverberate within the frenzied moral dilemmas of the city.

Miller consistently positions his characters in precise urban constructs in which the speeches of those characters seem singularly and unmistakably metropolitan. However, when the auditor of those vocalizations listens carefully to the contexts of the dialogue, and when the psychological foundations of the words become evident, then the urban and concrete shadows that seemingly minimize the speeches begin to expand and spread, pointing to a grander expanse where the syllables and the innuendoes of Middle America lie.

Works Cited

Bakhtin, M. M. *The Dialogic Imagination: Four Essays.* Austin: University of Texas Press, 1981.

Bigsby, C. W. E. *Modern American Drama 1945-2000.* Cambridge: Cambridge University Press, 2000.

————. *A Critical Introduction to Twentieth Century American Drama.* Cambridge: Cambridge University Press, 1984.

Centola, Steven. "Compromise and Bad Faith: Arthur Miller's *A View from the Bridge* and William Inge's *Come Back, Little Sheba.*" *Midwestern Quarterly* 28.1 (1986): 100-13.

Cohn, Ruby. *Dialogue in American Drama.* Bloomington: Indiana University Press, 1971.

Curtis, Penelope. "Setting, Language, and the Force of Evil in *The Crucible.*" In *Twentieth Century Interpretation of* The Crucible. Edited by John H. Ferres. Englewood Cliffs, NJ: Prentice-Hall, 1972. 67-76.

Derrida, Jacques. *Of Grammatology*. Baltimore: Johns Hopkins University Press, 1976.

Miller, Arthur. *The Crucible*. New York: Penguin, 1952.

———. *Death of a Salesman*. New York: Penguin, 1949.

———. *Echoes Down the Corridor: Collected Essays 1944-2000*. Edited by Steven Centola. New York: Penguin, 2000.

———. *The Price*. New York: Penguin, 1968.

———. *The Theater Essays of Arthur Miller*. Edited by Robert A. Martin. New York: Viking, 1978.

———. *A View from the Bridge*. New York: Penguin, 1955.

Otten, Terry. *The Temptation of Innocence in the Dramas of Arthur Miller*. Columbia: University of Missouri Press, 2002.

Pradhan, N. S. *Modern American Drama: A Study in Myth and Tradition*. New Delhi: Arnold-Heinemann Publishers, 1978.

von Szeliski, John. *Tragedy and Fear: Why Modern Tragic Drama Fails*. Chapel Hill: University of North Carolina Press, 1971.

Figuring Our Past and Present in Wood: Wood Imagery in Arthur Miller's *The Crucible* and *Death of a Salesman*

William Smith

In his works, Arthur Miller repeatedly examines humankind's battle against a flawed society, often describing society as impersonal, profit-driven, and overpoweringly commercial. Within these examinations, Miller skillfully manipulates images of nature, working their colors and connotations into a backdrop for his larger critical assessment of contemporary America and its inherently destructive powers. This application of pastoral imagery features innovative wood figurations, employed with great variety and success. For Miller, wood resides at the heart of early American life and represents the instinct to escape the machinations of an increasingly industrial society and return to what one knows best and what one knows **is** best—living in nature and working with one's own hands, ultimately generating a transcendental satisfaction not otherwise attainable. Through a complex application of his wood trope, Miller suggests that to survive within, and succeed against, the self-effacing pressures of a dominant and destructive modern culture, each person must find a way to connect with his/her natural past through wood and manual labor.

Despite their apparent dissimilarities, two of Miller's greatest plays are united in their exposure of a broad spectrum of the playwright's figurations of wood. In the historical drama, *The Crucible*, Miller connects characters like John Proctor, Giles Corey, and even Francis Nurse to the wood that is central to colonial village life. These are also characters who challenge the fundamentalism of Puritanism, a belief system, as presented by Miller, rife with flaws and available to corruption. In *Death of a Salesman*, set in a time when society is no longer wood-based, Miller ties wood to Willy Loman's pastoral longings and his desire to work with his hands. A thematic objective of the play is realized when the wood of the natural world meets the bricks and glass of the modern society, which, like the Puritan religion, is cold, impersonal, and without the natural elements necessary for the survival of the common man (here, Willy and Biff Loman). While Miller's wooden figurations in these two works range from forest to lumber pile, they unite to serve Miller's larger examination of the society's threat to individuality.

Salem's historical setting establishes and bolsters Miller's thematic objectives for *The Crucible*. Nestled between the ocean and the largely unexplored forestland of seventeenth century America, Salem provides a natural and symbolic backdrop for the play. Miller recognized the symbolic value of the land, and in the *Overture,* describes the new land as the "barbaric frontier" (135), adding, "The American continent stretched endlessly west, and it was full of mystery for them. It stood, dark and threatening, over their shoulders night and day, for out of it Indian tribes marauded from time to time, and Reverend Parris had parishioners who had lost relatives to those heathen" (135). These remarks foreshadow the actions that take place in the woods and emphasize the Puritan fear of nature uncontrolled.

Miller's description of the land becomes the foundation for many of his figurations. Forests (wood [nature] in its most pure and unadulterated state) are matched continually against the "unnatural" Puritan society. The forest, literally and figuratively, represents the boundary of Puritan theology. Inside the untamed forests, Puritanism meets, and in many regards is defeated by, its greatest opposition— the devil's temptations. Characters in the play conflict over possession of the forestland (decidedly un-Puritan behavior) and conduct unholy rituals there. The heathenish dancing of Abigail and the girls, for example, takes place in the forest, as does Abigail's secret meeting with Proctor later in the play. Not surprisingly, "Salem folk believed that the virgin forest was the Devil's last preserve, his home base and the citadel of his final stand. To the best of their knowledge, the American forest was the last place on earth that was not paying homage to God" (136).

Because wood and forests connect to the Puritans' assessment of their own success at creating and maintaining a society completely free from sin, Miller's wood figurations represent the Puritan attempt to bolster its own waning sense of security (historically, Puritanism was somewhat short-lived, perpetually struggling to maintain its foothold). Because the wild forestland is Puritanism's enemy, any opportunity to demonstrate control over the wilderness is taken and flaunted publicly. In essence, "good" Puritans battle against the wilderness as they would against the devil. Accordingly, Miller emphasizes such attempts, as evidenced in the power struggles over land ownership—the rights to deforest the land. Cleared or controlled (farmed) land is land without the devil or temptation to sin. These land struggles involve stakes far higher than merely acreage. Since religion dictated law in Puritan society, and since deforested land represents a show of religious strength, one can logically conclude that products derived from, or activities connected to, that deforestation would be of great significance to the community. Miller remarks in his *Overture*, "Land-lust which had been expressed by constant bickering over boundaries and deeds, could now be elevated to the arena of morality; one could cry witch against one's neighbor and feel perfectly justified in the bargain" (137-38). In Miller's Puritan world, moral battles are won often by those viewed most favorably by the church. Because the church represents the legal authority in a theocracy, struggles over land and wood are demonstrations of one's power and, perhaps, one's Puritan convictions. He who can possess and clear the most land is in some way the strongest Puritan because he rids Salem of acres of heathenish temptation.

Many characters enter such land-lust struggles. The most powerful of these men is Thomas Putnam, a man who had been on the losing side of a ministerial appointment in Salem and who had been trying to re-establish his importance in the town—largely with his weakly founded assertions of land ownership. Putnam battles over wood/land with Giles Corey, John Proctor, and Francis Nurse during the play. These land battles—because they represent a measure of Puritan faith—become "elevated to the arena of morality" (137). In this arena, Nurse pays the price for challenging the powerful Putnam when Goody Putnam vindictively charges Rebecca Nurse with witchcraft, proving that anyone can be victimized when someone wishes to pervert the religion.

When Putnam challenges Proctor's rights to get lumber from a certain tract of land, the greater significance of Putnam's power-play appears. Proctor, a man who has "a sharp and biting way with hypocrites...strong of body, even tempered, and not easily led" (148), a man who is at odds with the church, and who symbolically exists outside of its bounds, represents a character to be feared. Because he is a freethinking Puritan, he threatens the control needed to uphold Puritanism. Connecting specifically to Miller's theme of wood and nature, John Proctor is one of the few characters who makes specific references to working with his hands out on his land. Proctor is an artist of sorts, free to be creative and inspired (he put the wooden roof on the church and hung its wooden door). An anomaly, he bridges the gap between the construct of Puritanism and the wholly heathenish man. Proctor and Nurse, and even to some extent Giles Corey, are men at once both Puritan and free thinkers. They challenge the artificiality in the construction of any society that puts a rigid framework upon natural existence. Ironically, both literally and figuratively, Proctor is destroyed by the very construct he challenges; he is hanged from the wooden Puritan gallows for standing against the hypocrisy of the church.

The land-lustful society also prizes the products of the forest. Reverend Parris, in a very non-Puritan expression of greed, sees wood as a powerful bargaining tool. "Where is my wood? My contract provides I be supplied with all my firewood....I am paid little enough without I pay six pound on firewood" (155-56). Miller extends his theme beyond firewood to the wooden beams of the courthouse. He describes the "heavy beams [that] jut out" (200) of the meeting house. Combined with the gibbet, a construction of which the villagers are certainly proud, the images suggest the villagers' pride in their ability to take trees from the heathen forest, master them, and shape them to fit their needs. The exposed beams of the meeting house, the debates over land and firewood, and even the wooden doors on the church and the meeting house represent modifications to the natural state of the trees as they would exist untouched in the forestland. Metaphorically, these elements echo the modifications to the "natural state" of humankind when it conforms to Puritanism.

When Miller addresses similar thematic issues in *Death of a Salesman*, he again figures wood with great variety to represent the tension created as the natural state of humans is matched against the modern world structure. In the setting of this work, society has moved away from wood toward brick, steel, and glass. The characters who possess an affinity for wood, wishing to handle it and build with it, are left in the past, vanquished by mainstream values. In this play, as in *The Crucible*, a character can attempt to bridge the natural and constructed worlds, but success is not certain. Though wood and other elements of nature can be manipulated to create value in the free-market, the process requires the sacrifice of nature and, as Willy demonstrates, perhaps of oneself.

Miller immediately establishes wood as a resonant symbol in *Death of a Salesman*. In the opening stage description, he depicts the "solid vault of apartment houses around the small, fragile-seeming home....Under and over it we see the apartment buildings....The entire setting is wholly or, in some places, partially transparent" (21). The towering, brick apartment buildings block sunlight from Willy's garden and overshadow his home. Their looming presence threatens the wall-less and beam-exposed house and all of its occupants. It is clear from the outset of the play that all things wood are on the verge of extinction. The modern man of brick and glass soon will replace the man of wood who wishes to live close to nature. Willy hints at his impending doom when he claustrophobically says to Linda,

> The way they boxed us in here.... Bricks and windows, windows and bricks.... There's not a breath of fresh air in the neighborhood.... They should've had a law against apartment houses. Remember those two beautiful elm trees out there? When I and Biff hung the swing between them? They should've arrested the builder for cutting those down. They massacred the neighborhood. (26)

Miller's immediate juxtaposition of bricks and wood provides the thematic foundation for Willy's tragic defeat at the hands of modern society.

Shortly after his remark about the lost trees, Willy introduces his sentiment which continues throughout the play and is shared, and perhaps embraced, more successfully by Biff—the desire to work with his hands, away from the city, immersed in nature. Willy tells Linda, "You wait, kid, before it's all over we're gonna get a little place out in the country.... I'd build a little guest house. 'Cause I got so many fine tools, all I'd need would be a little lumber and some peace of mind.... I could build two guest houses" (73). Here, wood represents Willy's salvation. If he can return to a world that respects his tool handling and his skill with wood, perhaps he can be happy.

Willy's son, Biff, shares some of Willy's sentiments. "Sure, maybe we could buy a ranch.... Men built like we are should be out in the open.... Because we don't belong in this nuthouse of a city! We should be mixing cement on some open plain, or— or carpenters" (31, 64). Both men refer to wood when speaking of their dreams. Willy's romantic longings for the pastoral suggest his desire to live in the country where there are trees rather than cleared lots and buildings. His dream also involves carpentry, a longing to work with his hands that re-appears throughout the play. The carpentry sentiment appears in Biff's speech as well. For reasons similar to his father's, Biff longs to be outdoors, with his shirt off, working close to the land.

Willy's desire to work with wood is given genetic history when the audience learns about his father's and brother's explorations of the landscape. Ben says, "Father was a very great and a very wild-hearted man. We would start in Boston, and he'd toss the whole family into the wagon, and then he'd drive the team right across the country. And we'd stop in the towns, and sell the flutes that he'd made on the way" (53). Similarly, Ben brags, "William, when I walked into the jungle, I was seventeen. When I walked out I was twenty-one. And, by God, I was rich!" (56). The jungles (masses of untamed woodlands) and the countryside, for Willy, represent the natural world to which he would like to escape, not the man-made world of his present life. However, unlike his brother and father, Willy lacks the vocabulary necessary to translate his dreams into a successful reality.

Though Willy idealizes the experiences of his father and brother, significant thematic points exist regarding their successes. Ben, like his father, is able to rape the land of its natural resources. This raping alone does not make him rich; unlike Willy, Ben is able to translate his "experience in nature" into modern terms and create a fortune. When Ben re-enters commercial society, his raw stones are cut to create valuable gems. Similarly, Ben's father constructs the wooden flutes from unrefined, natural resources and then finds markets in which to sell them. In both instances, the men are able to enter forests, take what they need, and successfully re-enter the materialistic world. Willy is unable to attain this goal.

Willy's father's connection to nature raises a concept of value that Miller revisits throughout the play. Biff's theft of lumber from the construction site of the apartment buildings leads Willy to gloat, "You shoulda seen the lumber they brought home last week. At least a dozen six-by-tens worth all kinds of money" (55). Ironically, the boys steal wood (nature) that had to be delivered into the city which, because of its uncontrollable construction, has very few trees remaining. But unlike Ben and Willy's father, the boys steal this lumber, adding to it no value of their own. Lumber has already been processed and ascribed a value, the same way Ben processed his natural stones to make them valuable, and his father processed raw wood into flutes to make them a commodity. The audience recognizes the difference between Ben and Biff, but, sadly, Willy does not.

Emphasizing the destructive power of modern society, Miller finds a multitude of ways to juxtapose society and nature. Ben offers Willy a job overseeing Alaskan timberland he has purchased, and Willy excitedly replies, "God, Timberland! Me and my boys in the great outdoors" (84). For Willy, the woods hold hope of great solace and peace. Both his relatives go to the woods to find happiness and ultimately great fortune. However, ultimately, each of these men finds his fortune as a salesman. Salesmen are a societal construct, a perversion of sorts, necessitated only by a capitalist society.

Willy's pastoral longings and desire for human brotherhood battle the profit-driven, "un-natural" society in additional lines that specifically reference wood or woodcraft. After becoming smitten with a new tape machine, Howard says, "I'm gonna take my camera, and my band saw, and all my hobbies, and out they go..." (79). If Miller created Howard as the prototypical businessman, then his discarding of the band saw predicts Willy's ruin; modernity will replace the wooden relic. Willy says earlier in the play to Charley, "A man who can't handle his tools is not a man. You're disgusting" (49). He also says about Charley, "Between him and his son Bernard, they can't hammer a nail!" (55). In a sense, the value placed by salesman Willy on handiwork casts him from the modern world. Willy seems aware of this somewhere in his mind, and his fear of incompatibility with modern values is ironically stated to Ben. "Sure, Sure. I am building something with this firm, Ben, and if a man is building something, he must be on the right track, mustn't he?" (84).

Regarding Biff, the nuances of wood become even more powerful. Describing the power of being well liked, Willy states, "You can't feel it in your hand like timber, but it's there" (85). Tragically, this comment reveals how Willy's business instinct fails him. The ideas which he believes can maintain him (being well-liked, naming a child, etc.) contain little value in a world that needs the tangible (profits, structures, contracts, etc.). When Biff appears suddenly to have thrown away his boyhood dreams, Willy tells Bernard that he "laid down and died like a hammer hit him" (91). In essence, a hammer does hit Biff. He realizes how unnatural the modern, sales-oriented society is.

Though the Lomans possess a streak of self-reliance, Willy chooses suicide to ensure Biff's success. Willy is dying as a result of his attempt to bridge two disparate and incongruous existences. He cannot enter the pastoral world completely and live like a frontiersman or give himself wholly over to the industrial world and succeed as a salesman. In a prophetic statement to the boys prior to his death, Willy seems to understand his dreams will never be realized: "I'm not interested in stories about the past or any crap of that kind because the woods are burning. . . . There's a big blaze going on all around" (103). This statement appears earlier in the drama during a conversation with Hap, when Willy insists his sons must pick up the torch, root themselves, and become productive: "Where are you guys, where are you? The woods are burning! I can't drive a car!" (47). The repeated line carries with it the urgency of Miller's wood trope. The burning woods represent the destruction of nature as the city is evolving and suburban sprawl is replacing the rural areas. But they also signify the destruction of natural man. There will be no more Willy Lomans. Perhaps Biff will proceed with his dreams, but it is clear that Hap will follow the salesman's path that killed his own father, and perhaps killed his uncle and grandfather. For Willy, the blaze marks the passage of time, and more important his eclipse and extinction as representative of the common man. As Charley summarily declares, "The only thing you got in this world is what you can sell" (94). If a man cannot sell or be sold, he holds little value in the modern economy.

Miller concludes his wood figurations with a wonderfully understated, "Hammering is heard from outside the house, off right. Biff turns toward the noise" (119). Biff is a character who runs from the paneled, wooden walls of Mr. Oliver's office in fear that his own dreams will be swallowed; who claims, "I saw the things I loved in this world. The work...and time to sit and smoke" (124); whose father praises his handiwork, bragging, "Biff can fell any one of those trees in no time" (54); whose father is fired across the wooden desk of a new generation of capitalists. Biff is instinctually drawn to the hammering because it is what he knows best.

Miller's figuration of wood in the two plays is brilliantly complex. While the wood imagery serves obvious functions, never arbitrarily featured in either play, it delicately transforms itself to meet Miller's specific needs. Occasionally, wood serves merely as a setting, carrying with it a symbolism established far before Miller's time. At other moments, wood is a part of the ecosystem of humankind's natural state, in which any unnatural variation represents the perversions forced upon nature by us. As raw material waiting to be crafted, wood draws us toward nature and away from the artificial world Willy both despises and tragically strives to join. In sum, the wood figurations combine to provide a framework for Miller's larger investigation of the theme of the difficult search for community.

One need not look any further than Miller's own life for the source of his fascination with wood, trees, and manual labor. Arthur Miller knows the satisfaction of pounding a hammer and drawing spiritual nourishment from wood and woodworking. Calling carpentry "his oldest hobby," Miller's own accounts make apparent the extent to which wood and crafting infuse his creative process. He describes in his autobiography how, prior to writing *Death of a Salesman*, he sought a space to write where he "could block out the world" (Miller, *Timebends* 183). That space turned out to be a small cottage that Miller designed and built himself as a writing workshop on the property of his farmhouse in rural Connecticut. Connected through wood to his childhood spent in a tree-lined neighborhood in Brooklyn, Miller appears to draw creative strength from the scent "of raw wood and sawdust" with which he surrounds himself to "block out" the modern world (Miller, *Timebends* 183) and to hearken back to a time in America's history where nature was enjoyed, if not revered, and manual labor and craftsmanship were part and parcel of human expression. Fortunately for Miller, he has avoided the fate of his characters John Proctor and Willy Loman and has found a way to successfully reconcile his attraction to the pastoral world and the economic and social realities of the modern world.

Works Cited

Miller, Arthur. *Death of a Salesman.* In *The Portable Arthur Miller.* Edited by Christopher Bigsby. New York: Penguin Books, 1995. 19-131.

————. *The Crucible.* In *The Portable Arthur Miller.* Edited by Christopher Bigsby. New York: Penguin Books, 1995. 132-258.

————. *Timebends: A Life.* New York: Harper & Row, 1987.

Damn Yankee! Leroy Hamilton Crafts Wood With Passion and Honesty, But Who in Modern America Cares?

William Smith

Arthur Miller's 1993 drama, *The Last Yankee*, reveals a playwright very focused on his thematic objectives. Hammering at the flaws inherent in a modern society which corrupts the natural instincts of the individual and forces upon him a mechanical and profit-driven culture to which he must adapt, Miller encapsulates the economic and social development of the American business world of the 1960s, 1970s and 1980s as it moved increasingly away from the manual labor market into high technology and corporate arenas. This evolution came with a price to be paid largely by the middle class.

Nowhere is this dilemma of the middle class more directly examined than in the life of Leroy Hamilton, the last of an American breed, a carpenter keenly aware of the public's scornful view of a tradesman's life. Like Miller's characters who have come before him (John Proctor, Willy Loman and Chris Keller), Leroy finds personal harmony in the natural landscape around him and the wood within that landscape that he manually crafts; but he realizes that to his family and the business-oriented world that surrounds him, his personal satisfaction has little value. To survive, he must ultimately be able to translate his passion into terms suitable to the established economic norms of the modern environment.

Appropriately, the visiting room of a state mental hospital is the setting for a play that raises questions about the emotional impact of the modern social and economic constructs upon those who endorse the system and those who attempt to buck it. In this room are powerful symbols of two disparate worlds. Leroy Hamilton, the last Yankee, a carpenter struggling to pay his bills each month and John Frick, a successful business mogul, sit opposite one another, each waiting for his hospitalized wife to join him. Immediately, Miller hints at which character deserves favor. Forty-eight year old Leroy, with suggestive irony, is described twice in the stage directions as "leafing" through a magazine, while sixty year old Frick, dressed in a business suit and carrying a valise, studies his watch and waits "impatiently." Leroy's pastoral roots insinuate themselves, as do Frick's bonds to the business world. From these opening descriptions, Miller develops these symbols and reveals the play's thematic charge.

Early within the exchange between the two men, Miller makes Leroy's incompatibility with the dominant culture clear. Though Leroy operates his own carpentry business, his traditional beliefs do not typify those of a modern businessman. Frick comments on Leroy's unusual "pride" and "independence," ironically citing that the rest of the world is plagued because "Everybody's got the gimmes, it's destroying the country" (Miller, *Yankee* 454). To Frick's surprise, Leroy reveals that despite his attire and well-heeled manner, he is "just" a carpenter who prefers to work alone rather than in the tiered corporate structure a contracting business would demand. In addition to shunning much of the modern business model, Leroy reluctantly acknowledges Frick's assertion that Leroy and his family "descended from Alexander Hamilton" (455). Frick finds this linkage significant perhaps because of Alexander Hamilton's role in shaping governmental economic policy and laying foundations for Wall Street economics. However, Leroy, like his father who "didn't care for [Hamilton's philosophy] much," says he only knows about Hamilton "more or less" (457), distancing himself from the economic legacy of his heritage—the legacy that currently dooms him.

Miller directly connects Leroy to the nation's colonial past, to wood and nature, to our founding fathers and to the traditional values of the frontiersman that Miller suggests are instinctive in mankind. Leroy is the manual laborer that John Proctor was and that Willy Loman longed to be. In contrast, Frick is the prototypical businessman, a former lumber yard owner who had frequently done business with Leroy but is unable to recall his face—though he lies to

Leroy's wife and tells her "I recognized your husband right away" (481). Identifying himself as a corporate entity—"By the way, I'm Frick Lumber" (481)—Frick personifies the corporation: impersonal and connected to wood only to the degree that he can turn a profit from it. He is the corporate figuration of Miller's wood trope, divorced from the hands-on connection that is so vital for Miller. Uninterested in the spiritual value of wood and craftsmanship, he "sold out" his lumber supply business to pursue a profitable fuel-oil business. Ironically both businesses co-opt natural resources, and, as seen earlier in *Death of a Salesman*, they offer little additional value to the product, merely leeching a fee from the customer for the transportation and inventory of the product.

In Leroy and Frick's conversation, several important facts appear. Leroy's most recent projects include a renovation of a colonial style house and a local Presbyterian church. Both projects connect Leroy to the frontier tradition. The "colonial" style house reminds us of Leroy's family tree, which includes one of the Founding Fathers. The work on the church, specifically his hand-crafted altar, directly connects Leroy's woodcraft to spirituality—specifically to the spirit of man that is inherent in manual labor. As Leroy's character unfolds, so does his contrast to Frick, the socially successful but spiritually bankrupt corporate symbol. Frick inquires about Leroy's past, asking how he found himself pursuing carpentry. When Leroy responds that he "just. . .liked it" (456) and that he was "just too dumb [to be a lawyer like his father] I guess" (456), Frick, bemused, searches for more information about Leroy's familial past, saying of the other Hamilton descendents:

> FRICK. —some of them must be pretty important people.
> LEROY. I wouldn't know. I never kept track of them.
> FRICK. You should. Probably some of them must be pretty big. (Miller, *Yankee* 457)

Frick implies that Leroy has wasted his forefathers' heritage, settling for a career in carpentry that shames his family name. The unspoken completion to his remark that other members of his family "must be pretty big" is that Leroy is not "big" or "important" at all. Frick's remarks expose his superficiality and money consciousness—traits not surprising given his occupation and career path. But more important to his character type, Frick reveals through his words the predominant social judgment of modern society. Though they feign appreciation for careers that involve manual labor, they really look down upon them—devaluing their own past as they devalue Leroy's present.

Leroy grows increasingly impatient as his conversation with Frick continues, remarking:

> LEROY. . . . I have to tell you that this could be what's
> driving so many people crazy.
> FRICK. What is!
> LEROY. This.
> FRICK. This what?
> LEROY. This whole kind of conversation. (458)

Leroy has heard Frick's judgmental remarks before, from other mouths. In his most compelling speech in the play, he exclaims against those like Frick:

> should I be ashamed I'm a carpenter? I mean everybody's
> talking 'labor, labor,' how much labor's getting; well if it's so
> great to be labor how come nobody wants to be it? I mean
> you ever hear a parent going around saying—*mimes thumb*
> *pridefully tucked in his suspenders*—'My son is a carpenter?'
> (458)

These angry words reveal Leroy's frustration with his current position. While he has no regrets about his choice, he barely makes enough money with his carpentry to support his family. Further, as the business world progresses down alternate paths, his trade is scorned as if a nuisance and an impediment to an individual's financial gains. Frick reveals this fact in offhanded remarks about a gentleman who came to change a showerhead in his home and shockingly charged seventeen dollars an hour. When Leroy later reveals that he makes seventeen dollars an hour for his carpentry, Frick, embarrassed, but with his characteristic attention to business goals responds, "if they'll pay it, grab it" (455).

The true extent to which Leroy is an individual fighting the overwhelming current against him appears in the second scene of the play, as it becomes apparent that even his wife shares Frick's judgment of him. In a conversation that typifies the majority's perspective of Leroy, she reveals several items about Leroy to Frick's wife, Karen. From her, we learn that "Yankees never sue," that "he can stick his head out the window and go high as a kite on a breath of fresh air," and most importantly that she's ashamed that ". . .at the same time he's absolutely refused to make any money, every one of our children has had to work since they could practically write their names" (462-63). Patricia's lines offer additional details about Leroy's character and reveal the irony found in the fact that much of society has abandoned the seemingly enviable self-reliant, natural, disciplined approach to living that he still embraces.

Patricia's incompatibility with her husband's values appears elsewhere in a series of remarks that reveal her to be little more than a materialist who has bought into the essential capitalist principles of consumerism—principles that keep men like Frick in business. She refuses "to ride around in a nine-year-old Chevrolet which was bought secondhand in the first place" (465) and resents that Leroy spends money on banjo lessons—a decision that likely adds to his spiritual development and connects him with the folk roots of America's past. Further, she becomes livid as "he's seriously thinking about donating his saw-and-chisel collection to the museum!—some of those tools are as old as the United States, they might be worth a fortune!" (464). As these women converse, one cannot help but realize that while Leroy plods along in the real world, these women are confined to a mental institution, each seeking treatment for a depression brought on because, "Anybody with any sense has got to be depressed in this country. Unless you're really rich, I suppose" (465).

As the women complete their lamentations about the state of the modern world, Patricia reveals some important information about her Swedish background. She discusses her husband's garden and describes the fate of her two brothers, Charles and Buzz. We learn that "Buzz hung himself on his wife's closet door" and "eight days later Charles shot himself on the tractor" (469). While seemingly insignificant, what Patricia offers about her brothers' lives is telling, and it illuminates Miller's expected endorsement of Leroy's character—one whose name derives from the French, "the king." We learn that Charles "won the All-New England golf tournament, and Buzz came within a tenth of an inch of the gold metal in the pole vault" at the Portugal Olympics (468). Later in their lives, they committed suicide due to "Disappointment" (469). The deaths of these men symbolize the effects of intense modern competition on the individual. Leroy reveals about his wife's family that competition was at the root of all of their troubles: "Each and every one of you

was automatically going to go to the head of the line just because
your name was Sorgenson. And life isn't that way, so you got sick"
(473). Both men were competitors, and without gleaning any internal
satisfaction from their charges, they opted to die, one on the back of
the tractor that connected him to the land that might have been able to
nurture him.

This fact is echoed in the conversation between the two women in
which Karen longs for the farming life of her past, admitting, "I wish
we could raise some vegetables like we did on the farm" (466). Her
comments are juxtaposed against a discussion of grocery stores—
conglomerates that reap the financial rewards of the growing and
harvesting of an increasingly smaller pool of individuals. This
example echoes the business model of other Miller characters, like
Ben Loman. The implication of the women's exchange is clear: the
current structure of society, dependent upon business and focused on
wealth, leads people inevitably toward an empty, depressed emotional
state from which only a connection to the organic can return them.

As the play continues, Leroy again becomes the focus, and with the
views of the majority of the world surrounding him solidly
established, his position as a bridge between two worlds becomes
clear. Leroy is a craftsman and not wholly comfortable with the
business aspects of his vocation; nevertheless, he attempts to bridge
the craftsman's and the businessman's world. The extent of this
bridging appears in items like the altar he handcrafts for the
Presbyterian church. Seeking his wife's approval of his savvy
business transaction, Leroy excitedly tells her that he "got Harrelson
to agree to twelve-thousand-five for the altar," to which his wife
responds, "and you were so glad to accept eight. . . . I just couldn't
help thinking of all these years wasted trying to get you to charge
enough" (471). At his wife's encouragement, Leroy overcharges for
the altar, reluctantly navigating the uneven moral landscape of the
contemporary business culture. The materialistic Patricia predictably
calls his decision "a wonderful thing" (471). It is clear that the sale
does not sit well with Leroy. Artificially raising the price on the altar
goes against his instinct and is forced upon him by economic realities.

With one foot tentatively placed in the stifling, immoral business
culture, Leroy more firmly plants his other foot within the organic
structure to which his love of wood and nature connects him. His
inability to conform to the accepted modern business practices creates
a rift between him and his wife who cannot fathom how Leroy can be
truly happy with his meager existence. Patricia cites Leroy's

"constant optimism" as a mere front for his own depression. She patronizingly remarks, "You've had no life at all, have you" (473). She charges, "You are depressed, Leroy! Because you're scared of people, you really don't trust anyone, and that's incidentally why you never made any money. You could have set the world on fire but you can't bear to work along with other human beings" (473). Patricia's assertions expose a certain incompatibility between Leroy and the mass of humanity. Leroy's lack of trust, which Patricia sees as a cognitive choice, is rooted in his personal experiences with modern men of questionable values who typify much of Miller's modern society. Leroy gives an example of attempts to share his workload dashed by violations of his trust: "The last human being I took on to help me tried to steal my half-inch Stanley chisel" (473). Most disappointing to Leroy is the fact that the criminal was a man who "has three grandchildren! And he's a Chapman—that's one of the oldest upstanding families in the county. . . . I mean God Almighty, they've had generals in that family. . ." (473). Leroy is stolen from by a man who is willing to jeopardize his family name for the monetary value of a tool.

Chapman, like Patricia who fears that Leroy will sell his antique tools to the museum, fails to see the intrinsic value of a woodcarving tool. Neither recognizes the deeper significance of Leroy's carpentry and the heritage to which his woodcraft connects him and conversely the modern culture from which it distances him. This modernity is typified by legacy-ignorant thieves and the comparable poor quality of modern tools. Leroy expects more from the men of the world than what they are willing to give him. For Leroy, traditional values and honesty outweigh any of his financial goals. Honor, tradition and character appear anathema to survival and success in economically-driven contemporary America.

The extent and impact of Leroy's bifurcation becomes more apparent as the dialogue continues and Patricia virtually forces Leroy to admit he is depressed and a "failure." In a revealing line exhibiting Patricia's frustration with Leroy, she sighs, "I feel like a log that keeps bumping against another log in the middle of the river" (474). By comparing each of them to logs, Patricia unknowingly alludes to *All My Sons* and the Kellers' apple tree—planted as a direct replacement of their son. Stripped of any other way to express to Leroy her bafflement at his rejection of the modern world, Patricia draws upon what Miller suggests resides in all of us—a spiritual connection to the wood-filled world of our frontiersmen forefathers.

Yet while she disavows her subconscious connections to the pastoral world around her (and faces the resulting depression), Leroy embraces it, hoping to escape momentarily from the construct and satisfy his soul. He lists for Patricia why his life is wonderful: "I mean the kids, and there are some clear New England mornings when you want to drink the air and the sunshine" (479). He later adds, "To me spiritual is whatever makes me forget myself and feel happy to be alive. Like even a well-sharpened saw or a perfect compound joint" (480). Despite his attempt to absorb himself in the craft that energizes his life and gives him spiritual satisfaction, Leroy inevitably faces the external pressures that force him to account economically for his actions. To each attempt at justifying his philosophy of life, Patricia counters with the representative voice of modernity, "You can make more out of a change in temperature than any human being I ever heard of—I can't live on weather. . . . I can't bear it when you can't pay the bills" (479). The ultimate result is that Leroy, too, faces a depression of sorts—a depression brought on by the essentiality of sacrifice to modern culture. At his core he is a partially defeated man, reluctantly accepting his lot in life because he sees no way around the financial pressures. He says, "But I'm a carpenter—this is probably the way it's been for carpenters since they built Noah's ark" (479).

As a bridge between two worlds, Leroy cannot find satisfaction in either sphere. His distrust of mankind and his distaste for seeing only the economic value in things, not their intrinsic, life-giving forces, saddens him and forces him to alienate himself from other workers and pull away from his wife. The satisfaction he might otherwise find in his craft is jeopardized by the economic realities that force him to overcharge for his work. The message is clear: crafting of the wood is fine, but as soon as one crafts with an eye on profit, he loses the joy in the activity, and it stops satisfying his soul.

Miller sets this play in the current reality—a world that has moved far beyond a dependence on wood and manual labor, but which pays lip service to the value of each while encouraging and rewarding a completely different economic reality. At one point, Leroy laughingly states, "Well all I hope is that I'm the last Yankee so people can start living today instead of a hundred years ago" (475). The emphasis in Leroy's words might likely be *start living today*, as he recognizes the fundamental flaw in modern economic structures—that in their absolute focus on earnings at any cost, they allow little space for the honor of tradition and the joy of manual labor. The end result is that he and his wife, for different reasons, become depressed. Patricia's depression is symptomatic of the effect of modern living on those who completely embrace its economic dictates. Those people, without any connection to the pastoral world around them, inevitably arrive empty and spiritually unsatisfied because they have abandoned what resides at the core of their human instinct. Leroy, while tied directly to the wood he lovingly crafts, becomes depressed because he cannot live and craft solely for the joy it brings him; instead he must bow to the economic pressures that mandate selling and consistently challenge his moral convictions. The painful acceptance of defeat in Leroy's words reveals how the dominant social and economic structures ostracized Leroy—not for his woodcraft, but rather for his inability to find a point of harmony between his own craft and the modern economic and technological realities that surrounded him and reduced the value of his manual talents.

Modernity is elastic and ever-changing. But for Miller, each era's modernity has included dominant, and in his view often detrimental, social and economic ideologies that have increasingly stripped Americans of the opportunity to create with our hands, to work with nature, and to connect to our pastoral heritage through crafting with wood. In his plays, Miller charts the evolution from wild forestlands with which man can communicate, to "those forests of canned goods high up near the sky. . .to which no human can reply" (Miller, "Birthday"), and concludes that only one forest can provide the raw materials to which Leroy Hamilton instinctively turns for sustenance. The closer one can get to a complete dissolution into the world of our ancestors, the less likely he will fall victim to the moral and economic pitfalls of modern social and economic structures. *The Last Yankee* provides disheartening evidence that the evolution of American society leaves a shrinking opportunity for the organic connection Miller argues is essential to well-being.

Works Cited

Miller, Arthur. *The Last Yankee*. In *The Portable Arthur Miller*. Edited by Christopher Bigsby. New York: Penguin Books, 1995. 447-88.

———. "The 'Salesman' Has a Birthday." *New York Times* 5 February 1950, sec. 2: 1,3.

"[S]omewhere down deep where the sources are": Traces of the Snyder/Gray Murder Trial of 1927 in *Death of a Salesman*?

Frank Bergmann

In his autobiography *Timebends* of 1987 Arthur Miller states the obvious, that "[n]o work of any interest has a single source" (223). Accordingly, he provides much information about personal experience of his that helped shape *Death of a Salesman*. Some of this experience he recalls with great clarity; at other times, however, he freely admits that he cannot recall a person's name or some fact of one kind or another. Even worse, once in an interview with Richard I. Evans and once in *Timebends*, he records major memory lapses regarding the genesis of that play. Gerald Weales has said that *Timebends* "is heavily marked with doctored memory" (647), and that may be so in certain instances, but at least as problematic for the scholar is, in Weales' words, that "details, including dates, become confused" (645). Everyone's memory is selective, but not every lapse may be traced to repression and denial; often enough a fact or an occurrence is simply not meaningful enough to be saved in some discrete cerebral file, though it certainly goes into the big memory pool for which Miller himself has used terms ranging from "boiling soup" to "sea" to "geological strata" to "somewhere down deep where the sources are" and from which from time to time details may rise and surface.[1] As a social playwright, Miller has always emphasized that a play must be connected to its time, and his autobiography amply demonstrates that he had his eyes and ears open from childhood on. Though Miller never mentions it, I want to suggest that the most notorious New York City murder case of 1927 left its traces in *Death of a Salesman*, and I want further to suggest how they got there.

On March 20, 1927, Ruth Snyder and her lover Judd Gray killed Ruth's husband Albert in the Snyders' house in Queens by bludgeoning him with a sash weight, chloroforming him, and garroting him with picture wire. They then messed up the house and left an Italian language newspaper lying around, and Judd rather loosely tied up Ruth, all in an effort to make it appear to the detectives that one or more Italians had burglarized the place and killed her husband in the process. Gray had arranged a fairly tight alibi back in Syracuse, where he happened to be staying at the Onondaga Hotel long enough to visit a close friend in town and go down to Queens and return after the murder. However, although they had become adept at cheating on their spouses for the better part of two years, the pair were inept criminals: Ruth's story was quickly pulled apart by the medical evidence and the investigation of the alleged robbery, and Judd dropped his train ticket into the wastebasket in his room in Syracuse where naturally it was found by the local police. Before the end of the second day, Ruth and Judd had signed detailed separate confessions. There is no need to say more about this matter except that it was the most publicized murder case of the year, went through all the stages of trial, verdict, sentencing, appeal, and petition for clemency, and ended on the electric chair in Sing Sing where Ruth Snyder and Judd Gray were executed on January 12, 1928.[2]

What are the traces of this case which I contend might well have found their way into Arthur Miller's most famous play? First of all, Judd Gray was a salesman; his territory was the Northeast, just like Willy Loman's, though it seems to have been larger, including upstate New York and Pennsylvania. Miller speaks of several salesmen in *Timebends*, foremost among them his two uncles in Brooklyn, Manny Newman and Lee Balsam. There was also a salesman friend of Manny's who told young Arthur, "'You've gotten serious,'" and of whom Miller says: "If I ever knew that salesman's name I forgot it long ago, but not his few interested words that helped crack the shell of suffocating subjectivity surrounding my existence" (127). Finally, there is the salesman, Schoenzeit, in Miller's unpublished sketch "In Memoriam" of 1932, "who committed suicide by jumping in front of a subway train" (Walden 190). In and of itself, then, Gray's being a salesman would seem immaterial, except that he was a corset salesman. In his admittedly imaginatively enhanced portrait of Gray, historian Karl W. Schweizer makes a great deal of that fact. Gray's description of his life as a salesman to the detectives who question him is suffused with eroticism: "'Women? Sure, I met plenty of them—on the road, in trains, restaurants, hotels, and I learned to place every type: the nice girl who flirts, the nice girl who does not, the flapper type and the out-and-out street walker my father warned me against—all sorts.' He smiled sheepishly, 'I guess I did flirt and drift a bit perhaps but Isabel—my future wife—was the only one in my heart'" (89). Equally evocative is Schweizer's rendering of Gray's rushed and often lonely life as a salesman (88), and just as pertinent for Willy Loman is the way Schweizer reconstructs Gray's testimony as to what makes a good salesman: "'One week on the road taught me the importance of personality: a hearty handshake, a cheerful smile—to be happy was the thing, no matter what, and often booze was the prescription'" (88). Quite early in their acquaintance, Gray made Ruth Snyder a present of a corset, an occasion which Schweizer develops erotically and uses to point out that Gray's firm was not only in corsets and girdles but also in lingerie (202-203). It is not really a present, as Gray charges it to stock (203). In the restaurant scene in Act Two of *Death of a Salesman*, Happy pretends to Miss Forsythe: "'I sell champagne, and I'd like you to try my brand.... It's all company money'" (*Collected Plays* I, 194). In Miller's scene directions at the very beginning of the play, Willy carries "two large sample cases" which surely are not only metaphorically heavy, as he "lets his burden down, feeling the soreness of his palms" (131). Miller never lets on what it is Willy sells; in the "Introduction" to *Collected Plays* he writes: "And when asked what Willy was selling, what was in his bags, I could only reply, 'Himself'" (28). The Woman in Boston is surely interested in Willy, but the fuss she makes is about "two boxes of size nine sheers" (207) which Biff considers "'Mama's'" (208). Willy can't stand it when Linda darns stockings, especially when he comes off a memory of giving the Woman in Boston new ones (150-51). One of the stores Willy mentions as being part of his beat, Filene's (166), is even today instantly recognizable as a major clothing department store. Perhaps, then, Willy's sample cases were not full of hot air like himself but of corsets and lingerie—and stockings.

Trial testimony, according to Schweizer, suggests that Gray was a momma's boy, "'[h]er only son, whom she adores" (66). Gray called Ruth "Momsie" not only in moments of passion (210) or distress (96) but used that appellation when he asked his friend in Syracuse to cover for him because he had a "dinner engagement with a certain lady" in Albany (98)—he was, of course, en route to Ruth in Queens. There seems to be conflicting testimony as to whether it was Judd or Ruth who garroted Albert Snyder, but this is what the neighbors and later the police found: "A picture-wire was looped around his throat, twisted with a metal pencil so tightly that the wire was barely visible beneath the folds of Albert's flesh" (2). As long ago as 1950, Daniel E. Schneider, M.D., elucidated the oedipal dynamics of the play, though certain comments by Miller in *Timebends* make clear that he would have found a sufficient model in himself. Still, Bill Oliver's fountain pen, which Biff steals (*Collected Plays* I, 197, 201), is as lethal to the Loman Brothers notion as the metal pencil was to Albert Snyder in the marital bedroom; further, Miller interweaves the telling of the Oliver episode with the flashback of Biff surprising his dad with the Woman in Boston.

Before Ruth Snyder found herself so much at the end of her rope that she decided to kill her husband with the help of her lover, she had attempted several times to rid herself of him by poisoning pudding or whiskey (on one occasion, he barely got out of the closed garage where he had left the car running). Twice Ruth disconnected the tubing from the gas heater pipe when Albert was taking a nap in that room (212, 218-19). In the play, it is, of course, Willy who tampers with the gas pipe to the water heater as one possible way to commit suicide. It is necessary to note, however, that in *Timebends*, Miller recalls accidents involving gas from his childhood, accidents which happened in his parents' Harlem home or near it (20, 49).

Finally, there is the insurance matter. In November 1925, Ruth Snyder talked Albert into taking out a $1,000 life insurance policy but asked the insurance salesman for additional blanks. These she completed for $5,000 and $45,000, with the larger one carrying a double indemnity in the event of accidental death. During the trial someone advanced the theory that she copied a trick of Cardinal Richelieu's from the movie *The Three Musketeers* in which Richelieu held three documents slightly staggered on top of one another, claiming they were one document that needed three signatures. She kept the policies, payments, and correspondence secret (211-12). During the trial, it was this insurance matter which gave the prosecution an open-and-shut motive for the murder of Albert Snyder (240). Linda Loman tells Biff that the insurance company has evidence that Willy's car accidents "'weren't—weren't—accidents'" (*Collected Plays* I, 164). In his altercation with Charley, Willy muses "'you end up worth more dead than alive'" (192), only to be corrected by Charley, but as the conclusion shows, Willy does not listen, likening his fraudulently obtained blood money (if indeed the insurance ever does pay up) to Ben's (equally bloody?) diamonds.

Why and how should any of the Snyder/Gray matter have come to Arthur Miller's attention? After all, Arthur turned only twelve at about the time of the appeal of the case in Albany, and he mentions the case neither in *Timebends* nor in any other instance I am aware of. One reason why he could not possibly have been ignorant of the case was its enormous and continuing publicity. In his chapter "The Ballyhoo Years" in *Only Yesterday*, Frederick Lewis Allen highlights the American public's appetite for sensational events and sensational reporting, an appetite which reached its height in the Snyder/Gray affair:

> In this case there was no mystery, nor was the victim highly placed; the only excuses for putting the Snyder-Gray trial on the front page were that it involved a sex triangle and that the Snyders were ordinary people living in an ordinary New York suburb—the sort of people with whom the ordinary reader could easily identify himself. Yet so great was the demand for vicarious horrors that once more the great Western Union switchboard was brought into action, an even more imposing galaxy of special writers interpreted the sordid drama (including David Wark Griffith, Peggy Joyce, and Will Durant, as well as Mrs. Rinehart, Billy Sunday and Doctor Straton), and once more the American people tasted blood. (215)

In the Miller household, Arthur's mother would have followed the story if his recollection of one particular penchant of hers is correct. He recalls in *Timebends* a chance meeting with his uncle's widow, Stella: "And all at once I saw that I had brought all her losses into the shop with me, including my recently dead mother, whom she had come to adore and who in so many ways was like her. They shared a lust for foul jokes, filthy punch lines, sex scandals, *relationships*, the whispered world of frank women and their scents" (35). Thus, it is hard to believe that Arthur should have heard or read nothing about the Snyder/Gray case. Another possibility is Miller's seeing later on the blockbuster movie *Double Indemnity*, a 1944 Billy Wilder film based on a novel by James M. Cain; Schweizer believes that some of Cain's work is based on the Snyder/Gray case (295). More likely is Miller's hearing about the case at home and then forgetting that he had. Quite incredibly, Miller admits to having forgotten two major influences on *Death of a Salesman*. Quoting from Richard I. Evans, *Psychology and Arthur Miller* (1969), Daniel Walden makes a point of Miller saying that after he had written the entire play, he came across an old college notebook from 1936 in which "'there was a play about a salesman of which I'd written an act and a half.... I had completely forgotten that I had written an act and a half of the play...'" (193). The other instance is reported at great length in *Timebends* (177-79). One afternoon, Miller stepped into a midtown movie theater to see Fritz Lang's *The Testament of Dr. Mabuse* which he had seen some years before: "I had been making preliminary sketches of scenes and ideas for a salesman play and should have been home at my desk. I was still at the stage of trying to convince myself that I could find a structural arch for the story of the Lomans, as I called the family. The name had appeared suddenly under my hand one evening as I was making my vagrant notes" (177). He rediscovers that the name of one of the characters in the movie is Lohmann: "My spine iced as I realized where I had gotten the name that had lodged so deep in me. It was more than five years since I had last seen the film, and if I had been asked I never could have dredged up the name of the chief of the Sûreté in it" (178-179).

The parallels I have claimed are not all weighty, nor are they all exact, but I submit that together they may have helped Miller shape for *Death of a Salesman* what he says of *All My Sons*, "the wonder" that arises out of "the thickest concentration of facts," the ability to tell "the story of the play to even an unlettered person and spark a look of recognition on his face" (*Collected Plays* I, 15). Who knows, perhaps other aspects of the Snyder/Gray case made their way into the "boiling soup" into which Miller has been dipping his ladle all these years. In *Timebends*, he speaks of an unfinished play from 1950 about "a group of research physicians employed by a wealthy pharmaceuticals maker who inspires them to important discoveries while suborning them to his business interests. . .. Into their midst comes the mistress of Dr. Tibbets, Lorraine, a character modeled rather distantly on Marilyn, whom I still barely knew" (326). Perhaps so distantly that naming the character "Norma" would have been too close. But why Lorraine? Is she, too, in Fritz Lang's movie? It so happens that Lorraine is the name of Albert and Ruth Snyder's daughter—but that is another story.

Notes

[1]For "soup" see James J. Martine, 178; for "strata" see *Timebends*, 586 and 590; for "deep down" see *Timebends*, 36. In September 1972, I inquired of Miller if he had derived some of his notions concerning great artists from Hesse's "immortals"; on November 1, he replied: "No Hermann Hesse, I'm afraid—although we're all in the same sea if not the same boat."

[2]All information regarding this case is from Karl W. Schweizer, *Seeds of Evil: The Gray/Snyder Murder Case* (N.p.: 1st Books Library, 2001).

Works Cited

Allen, Frederick Lewis. *Only Yesterday: An Informal History of the Nineteen-Twenties.* New York and London: Harper, 1931.

Martine, James J. "'All in a Boiling Soup': An Interview with Arthur Miller." In *Critical Essays on Arthur Miller.* Edited by James J. Martine. Boston: G. K. Hall, 1979. 177-88.

Miller, Arthur. *Arthur Miller's Collected Plays.* Vol. 1. New York: Viking , 1957.

———. *Timebends: A Life.* New York: Grove, 1987.

———. Letter to author, 1 November 1972.

Schneider, Daniel. *The Psychoanalyst and the Artist.* New York: Farrar, Straus, 1950.

Schweizer, Karl W. *Seeds of Evil: The Gray/Snyder Murder Case.* N.p.: 1st Books Library, 2001.

Walden, Daniel. "Miller's Roots and His Moral Dilemma: or, Continuity from Brooklyn to *Salesman.*" In *Critical Essays on Arthur Miller.* Edited by James J. Martine. Boston: G. K. Hall, 1979. 189-96.

Weales, Gerald. "Arthur Miller and the 1950s." *Michigan Quarterly Review* 37 (1998): 635-51.

The Late Plays of Arthur Miller: Problematizing the Real

Ashis Sengupta

Reality is more problematic in the plays of Arthur Miller than has been generally conceded. In the early work, the real—clouded by personal delusions and public myths—eventually shines out with one's acceptance of responsibility for the consequence of one's own action. The sixties plays, which brought Miller back to the American stage after a long hiatus, question this version of reality by discovering evil in the depths of the self. Yet his moralism continues as he looks for redemption in one's ultimate recognition of complicity. But in the later plays beginning with *The Archbishop's Ceiling* (1977 [1989]), the real is "beyond either simple definition or full recovery" (Bigsby, *Modern American Drama* 84). With his increasing probe into the complexities of the postmodern condition, Miller has, on his own admission, "become more and more fascinated by...the question of reality and...whether there is any" (qtd. in Royal National Theatre 11). If *Archbishop* shows the problem of authentic behavior under the pressure of invisible power, *Two-Way Mirror* (1984) presents the unreal "as an agony. . .to be accepted as life's condition" (Miller, "Author's Note" 3). If *Danger: Memory!* (1986) questions the human capacity to generate systems to order experience and with it the traditional notion of representation, *The Ride Down Mount Morgan* (1991) dramatizes personal history as a narrative constructed from the fragments of memory and desire. And *Broken Glass* (1994), the last of the plays under discussion, deals with the mystery of a sociopolitical dilemma which threatens one's sense of reality.

No texts are without contexts and subtexts. The same is true of Miller's late plays. The Vietnam war and its aftermath, the Watergate scandal eroding people's faith in social systems, the repression of liberal freedoms of speech and artistic expression in 1970s Prague, the narcissistic culture in Reagan's America, ethnic conflicts in 1990s Yugoslavia—few of these issues directly figure in Miller's late work, but each has impinged upon his treatment of morality, and of reality too, as the question of reality, for him, is "a moral issue, finally" (qtd. in Royal National Theatre 11). With the myths of personal and public integrity crumbling all around, Miller lost faith in abstract virtues. As president of International PEN, he traveled extensively and found that "intellectual life in the whole developed world had been stunned by a common failure to penetrate Power with a…humane and rational point of view" (Introduction vii). He realized that the powers that be constitute the concepts, oppositions and hierarchies of a society's discourse, determining what would be accounted knowledge and truth. History, he admitted, is largely a myth created and destroyed "at the same time" to serve psychological and political needs. "It's very difficult to find the truth of the past," Miller said in a 1995 interview, because we can never "reconstruct ourselves truthfully" ("The Last Yankee" 94-95). His late plays throw into doubt his longstanding assumptions of an integral self and an integrated society. Now selves are seen to be in continuous construction. Each reality of self, to borrow Kenneth Gergen's phrases, "gives way to reflexive questioning, irony and ultimately the playful probing of yet another reality" (7). What had earlier passed for an unproblematic reality is no longer clearly distinguishable from its representations. In the absence of stable realities and values, any certainties the characters seem to have are at best positional since they are derived from what Linda Hutcheon would call "complex networks of local and contingent conditions" (12). With the testing of selves and truths, meaning becomes indeterminate and provisional in Miller's late plays. The "enormous variety of experience today," he says, is like "cornflakes…collapsing meaninglessly around our ears" (Miller, "A Conversation" 163). Miller's later work probes the ironies of contemporary life with an amused tolerance.

The dictatorial operation of power in 1970s Czechoslovakia and the expulsion of Solzhenitsyn from Russia, among other things, gave Miller the subject for *The Archbishop's Ceiling*. In Prague, with the Soviet ousting of Alexander Dubček and the repression of the intellectual opposition as spearheaded by Vánclav Havel, attempts at liberalization and reform came to naught. In his 1989 Introduction to the play, Miller describes the seventies as "the era of the listening device, government's hidden bugs set in place to police the private conversations of its citizens—and not in Soviet areas alone" (viii). "The White House was bugged," Miller adds, and Watergate and the publication of Pentagon Papers "demonstrated that "the Soviets had little to teach American presidents about domestic espionage" (Introduction viii). Thus, while Miller found himself in eastern European living rooms with ceilings bugged by the ruling regime, "it was not, disturbingly enough, an absolutely unfamiliar sensation for [him]" (Introduction viii). *Archbishop* asks, to put it again in Miller's words, what happens when "Power everywhere ... transform[s] itself from a forbidding line of troops into an ectoplasmic lump," or "when people know that they are—at least most probably, if not certainly – at all times talking to power" (Introduction vii, x).

What robs both life and art of all meaning is power, which in this play is located in the arbitrary functioning of the government of an eastern European country (clearly Czechoslovakia). The current regime claims to be more lenient, granting privileges and conveniences unavailable earlier. In return, it demands absolute compliance from people because it thinks itself an ideal form of government. But idealism may be totalitarian, as Lyotard would argue, in that it formulates prescriptive statements in reference to a determinate idea of the "good" and precludes all possibilities of dissent and dispute (22). The ceiling of the former archbishop's residence (now government-owned) is presumably bugged—which turns the writers, who collect under it, into compulsive actors. Coping with the state surveillance, or conformity to the state authority, seems to be the only option they are left with. Sigmund, the dissident novelist who appears to have been modeled on Havel, stands out against all compromises. But his action ironically contributes to the state's secret design to paralyze his will. The manuscript of his literary masterpiece, which assaults the ruling regime, has been confiscated by the government. Sigmund says: "Our country is now a theatre, where no one is permitted to walk out, and everyone is obliged to applaud" (69). His predicament becomes more awkward as the government promises to return the manuscript only if he goes into exile. If he flees, he loses the battle. If he does not, he may never get back the manuscript which contains for him the truth about his country. The government thus fictionalizes his moral stance in one way or the other. The new gods are the creators of fiction, as Bigsby says, and life under the archbishop's ceiling turns into theater as action dissolves so easily into performance (Afterword 91-92).

Adrian, the American writer who has come to this foreign turf to collect "truths" for his new novel, also ends up casting "life and fiction in a power struggle that unsettles...[his] assumptions" (Schlueter and Flanagan 126). He advises Sigmund to leave "this goddamned country" and also resolves to publicize the barbarous act of confiscation with the help of US Congress. But he loses his stand as he becomes suspicious about the ceiling which might have already recorded his protest. He has to counterfeit his speech immediately lest it jeopardizes Sigmund's safety: "I didn't mean that about the country" (77). Turned into a contrived self under the ceiling, Adrian cannot help Sigmund out of the impasse, however honest his intention may be. He is not sure either whether Marcus and Maya are secret service agents or friends to the writers whom they have assembled in the archbishop's room. Adrian seeks to know them better because they appear as major characters in his new book, but each remains as elusive as the ceiling until the end. Thus the issue is not only that freedom is denied, openly or otherwise, but that knowledge and writing become problematic in a world of compulsive performance.

More interestingly, one may have to generate private fictions, as Bigsby observes, in order to vie with the public ones (*A Critical Introduction* 235). Sigmund cannot define himself unless he invents his moral superiority. If Marcus is to be believed, the dissident refuses to leave not only for his pursuit of truth but for his own "monument," for "the bowering ushers in the theatre," for "the power...to bring down everyone" (89). No wonder he feels a mixture of joy and despair at the prospect of the release of his manuscript. Adrian also seems to have invented a moral relevance of his return. He thinks he is here to save Sigmund. But Adrian's concern for the confiscated manuscript is no less a concern for the story he himself is writing. Even Sigmund doubts Adrian's integrity and accuses him of pretending engagement when he is secure in his reputation. The charges point to "the theatricality that seems to be the only form of behavior possible in this arena" (Schlueter and Flanagan 132). None of the writers can be any more real outside than under the ceiling. The hidden microphones finally become a metaphor for what Miller calls "the bugged ceiling of the mind" to which we are always secretly talking for personal gains (*Timebends* 573). This calls into question the authenticity of commitment itself, political or artistic.

Miller's preoccupation with the elusive quality of reality also informs the four one-act plays of the eighties. *Elegy for a Lady* (1982) and *Some Kind of Love Story* (1983) are described by the author as "passionate voyages through the masks of illusion to an ultimate reality" ("Author's Note" 3). In the first play, the search is for "the shape and meaning of a sexual relationship that is being brought to a close by a lover's probable death" ("Author's Note" 3). In the second, "it is social reality and the corruption of justice which a delusionary woman both conceals and unveils" ("Author's Note" 3). However, in each, it is easier to identify "the masks of illusion" than to arrive at the "ultimate reality" Miller speaks of. Later, the very substance of reality now dissolves as character proves unstable. Later published as a double bill titled *Two-Way Mirror* (1984), the plays take us into "a world of images [and]...appearances in which things are not quite what they seem" (Bigsby, *Modern American Drama* 118). Realities, if there are any, are "refracted through memory. . .and self-concern," resulting in a wilderness of mirrors (118).

In *Elegy*, an older man enters a boutique, seeking a gift for his ailing young lover, which will not remind her of her mortality. Unable to choose it himself, he accepts the proprietress's suggestion of an antique watch which the dying woman might like to keep "exactly as it is ... forever" (19). The question of what to give sustains the dramatic action, June Schlueter correctly maintains, "but *Elegy for a Lady* subtly and suggestively questions more" (161). Is the woman really dying? Does the Man love her? Are both of them real or roles they have adopted to understand each other better? Is the Proprietress the lover in question? The Man only knows that his lover has a tumor, for which she is scheduled for surgery soon, and that she is depressed. His inference from such a premise about her impending death may or may not be correct, but it is what presently sets him pondering over the nature of the coming loss. Interestingly, the Man is "still unable to understand" if there is any love between them at all (12). In his conversation with the Proprietress he is perhaps trying to talk himself into a position and thus define his own feelings about his lover. As "the objective world grows dim and distant," says Miller, reality seems to consist of what the character's "needs require it to be" and the play turns out to be a monologue (*Timebends* 590). If the Proprietress is the lover herself who exists in the Man's mind, then both characters on stage are roles the Man has invented to understand the reality of his emotional moment. But this raises yet another teasing question. Does the role assumed by a person express an authentic self or leave the central self untouched? Since the play ends on a note of unresolved grief, notwithstanding the smile on the Man's face, role-playing fails to bring home to him the truth about his relationship with the absent woman. Significantly, neither the Man nor the Proprietress ever comes to know the other's name. *Elegy* is "an attempt to write a play," Miller says, "with multiple points of view ... like the neutrality of experience itself" (*Timebends* 589).

While *Elegy for a Lady* centers round an experience that evades definition for the indeterminacy of emotional as well as circumstantial truth, *Some Kind of Love Story* proceeds as a detective story which, paradoxically enough, fails to put together the details of a crime in the absence of social certainties and the psychological consistency of the prime witness. Though socially situated and realistically set, *Love Story* creates "a double vision of a reality to be distrusted but accepted" (Bigsby, *A Critical Introduction* 238-39). Former lovers Tom and Angela meet to discuss a murder case which Tom has been investigating for five years. Angela, the detective believes, can provide some vital clues that will help him get the innocent Felix out of jail. She tells Tom something of what she knows but will not reveal the whole truth. Nor are we sure if Angela has fabricated the crime story just to keep him near at hand. Though unsure about the motives of his witness, Tom cannot give up the case because the details Angela has already given out suggest a corruption so deep as to shake the very foundation of US law and justice.

In the Fall of 1973, Miller received a reprint of a *New York Times* article which contained extracts from a Connecticut state police interrogation of Peter Reilly, an eighteen-year old who had "confessed" to the brutal murder of his mother, and an appeal from the convict's neighbors to help clear the boy who was actually innocent. Though the boy was ultimately saved, the whole experience left Miller shattered. For it threatened his "idea of the law" as "the ultimate social reality, in the sense that physical principles are the scientist's ground—the final appeal to order, to reason, and to justice" (*Timebends* 584). Inspired by the incident, presumably, *Love Story* seems to ask: what if rational inquiry dissolves in a world of criminal conspiracy and possible paranoia? What if the motives of even those responsible to investigate are suspect? The answer implicit in the play is that it "destabilise[s] the very idea of reality" (Bigsby, *A Critical Introduction* 239). Miller describes Angela as both "dedicated to clearing an innocent man and possibly implicated in his having been condemned" (*Timebends* 590). During the grilling she confesses to her earlier affairs with three of the major suspects in the case—the police chief, the murdered drug dealer, and the prosecutor. But when she comes close to telling the truth about the possible criminal involvement of the city's political heavyweights, she slips into a series of alternate personalities: an eight-year-old girl, a street-corner whore, a sophisticated lady. Tom knows that she is hiding behind her old masks since he met her several times before in connection with the case, but he is not sure when he is seeing "*her real self*" (13). If Angela truly suffers from multiple personality disorder, then all these identities are pure delusions. But "could a person have delusions," as Tom asks his psychiatrist, "but like inside the delusion is the facts?" (15). Tom cannot confirm what he presumes. Moreover, he cannot fully trust Angela even when she sounds sane or seems to be cooperating with him. What, for example, causes her sudden concern for the prosecutor when she claims to be committed to freeing Felix? "Angela, whose side are you on?"—asks Tom (35). Angela cannot define herself, to borrow Miller's phrases, "because [when] the moral situation is so nebulous…few people can ever know what side they're on, or if there are sides" ("Just Looking" 94). This is an instance of a psychosis, says Bigsby, which is "as much that of a culture as of the individual who bears its marks" (*A Critical Introduction* 238). To quote Tom, the situation is "unreal," "horrendous[ly]" mysterious (39). As a "detective" story, the play is an ironic comment on rational inquiry in a world devoid of any criteria of veracity.

Dealing with the pain of recollection, caused as it were by the loss of youthful ideals, *Danger Memory!* (1986), another pair of one-act plays titled *I Can't Remember Anything* and *Clara*, seek to capture the mood of post-World War II America. *I Can't Remember* is a half-hour conversation between two aging friends, Leo and Leonora. The distance between the present and the past inevitably conditions their ability to recall and relate. However, disillusionment—not age—seems to be the ultimate cause for at least Leonora's amnesia and mediates her telling. She can perfectly remember some interesting events of her personal past; but she finds it hard to "remember anything political" (12). Yet the conversation between Leo and Leonora mostly centers around the degeneration of American life. The horrors that haunt them, says Rich, "are the same specters that hung over *After the Fall* and *Incident at Vichy*": police inquisitions, pogroms, and wars. But "characters of Miller's American generation," adds the critic, now painfully remember fragments of "history's cataclysms" as well as of "their own liberal crusades to ask what, if any, good came of it all" (Rich C15). The answers they find are at best ambiguous.

Ronald Reagan's victory represented the culmination of a growing reaction against the failed policies of American liberalism. But his popularity started declining after the Iran-Contra story broke in October 1986, the year the play was published, its "*time* [being] *now*" (*I Can't Remember* 3). The Reagan administration lied to Congress and the American people about the arms sale in Iran, and the president's obsession with Nicaragua reminded many Americans of Vietnam that he ironically wanted to leave behind. On the domestic front, again, when Reagan left office he left the American economy in a massive trade deficit. Though the play bears no direct reference to such events, they are implicit in Leonora's skepticism: "Why, our lives, the whole damned thing....that stupid newspaper with the same vileness everyday, the same brutality, the same lies..." (23-24). Terry Otten's analyses, in *The Temptation of Innocence*, of Miller's 1980s one-act plays trace the loss of innocence in characters who are looking for a moral position in a world less sure of its center. True. Leo finds it difficult to give up his quest finally. But Leonora recoils from that world lost as it is in "greed and mendacity" (24). Together, they represent a generation sandwiched between a past that belied high hopes and a present that makes the real unreal, the unreal real in order to hide its moral bankruptcy. While the past is almost obliterated for Leonora, her present is neither anchored to any concrete experience. At times she comes to doubt her own reality in this state of what Miller sarcastically calls "magic realism" (qtd. in Langteau 5): "I wonder if *I'm* imaginary" (9). Her inability to distinguish between authentic experiences and simulations is so characteristic of our age of disillusionment, "trauma and forgetting" (Melley 106).

Clara, the companion piece, is another detective story by Miller, in which reality is no less elusive than in *Some Kind of Love Story*. Albert Kroll's discovery of his murdered daughter's body in her apartment-office unnerves him before the interrogation of the investigating officer. Like Tom in *Love Story*, Detective Fine uses all his tricks to extract information from Kroll, the only person to have clues to the identity of the prime suspect. But Kroll cannot remember the name of the person because to remember, in his case, would be to confirm a suspicion, which would amount to questioning his self-reality. The failures of memory and identity thus operate on a profound sense of self-division—"a sense that one's experience can be secret even to oneself" (Melley 106). Kroll had handed the growing Clara some of his early idealism, which looms now as the ultimate cause of her death. Clara was working with former prisoners to reform and rehabilitate them. Though there is no prima facie evidence against the suspect, the likelihood is that the killer is one of those men, particularly one with whom she was in love. Though Clara told her father that the man had served a term for murdering his former girlfriend, Kroll could not oppose the relationship as it would challenge the validity of his own liberal past. But is Kroll the same person as he was when he staked his own life in Biloxi, Mississippi, to save the black men under his command from an angry lynch mob?

In the past twenty years, Miller writes in *Timebends*, Kroll has lost his "ideal ..., along with ... his faith in people" (591). The murder of his daughter confronts him with that ideal again. Must Kroll finally "disown" his ideal and "suffer guilt..." for having misled his child?— wonders the playwright "Or, despite everything," should he accept Clara's sacrifice as validating "the ideal" and his former "faith"? (*Timebends* 591) Critics complained that the ambiguity of the play would disappoint the audience. But the ambiguity instead reflects the contemporary mood—doubts about the grandly moral. An act can be morally right and wrong at once. It can be right to the extent that it contributes to a value, wrong to the extent that it detracts from another. Kroll's "approval" of Clara's mission was right, but he failed to convince his daughter that she should have proceeded with some caution. What may ultimately determine the rightness of an act over its wrongness, as May observes, is "the relative weights of the values" which it contributes to or detracts from and "the amount of [the] contribution and detraction involved" (91). But there are cases, like Kroll's, in which it is difficult to offer an account of relative weights or of relative contribution and detraction. This is the reason why Kroll finds the whole situation "so unreal" (40). He finally remembers the name of the probable murderer, proof that he has not fully given up his ideal, but he now finds the unpleasant consequence of a well-intentioned act as much real as the act itself. In Miller, action is always followed by consequence; but here one's ideal, not one's crime, becomes the source of a moral conflict. The effect is another relativist perspective on reality. The play possibly asks how to construct an account of moral practice as a contingent and yet compelling task.

Miller's fascination with the complexities of truth acquires yet another dimension in *The Ride Down Mount Morgan* (1991).

Circumstantially forced to examine his past, a man ends up as multiple selves beneath which we find no constancy. He is a poet, materialist, progressive, bigamist—all rolled into one. In is essay, "Miller in the Nineties," Bigsby quotes at length Miller's description of the play and its protagonist. Miller describes Lyman Felt as "a man of high integrity but no values." And it is a great paradox. For Miller, the play is "an attempt to investigate the immense contradictions of the human animal," to "look at ... [one's] limitless capacity for self-deception and for integrity." Lyman Felt does create "a socially responsible corporation" which has liberal policies toward minorities. But he is also "intent on not suppressing his instinctual life, on living fully in every way possible." He will "confront the worst about himself and then proceed from there." And "[t]hat is the dilemma," Miller notes, which is just "laid out in front of us" with "no solution to it" (qtd. in Bigsby, 171-72). Metaphorically, the accident Lyman meets with blows off his cover and necessitates a scrutiny of his past. However, it is far from an objective reconstruction as the past is presented to us through the unreliable memories and fantasies of Lyman. His present, too, is largely shaped by his fevered visions or conscious rationalizations. Since he inhabits a world he invents, and the others in it are but projections of his desires and fears, the real is no more stable here than in the above plays.

With his rising fear of death (symbolically suggested by Lyman's dead father carrying a black shroud-like cloth to cover his son with), the successful Lyman begins to enjoy life at the cost of all logic and morality. Unlike Eddie Carbone of A View from the Bridge (1956), a loving husband who cannot however face the reality of his unbridled passion for his niece, Lyman, though committed to his wife Theo, not only accepts his extramarital affair with the younger Leah on its own terms but finally transforms it into a bigamous marriage without their knowledge. Convinced that it is the only possible way for all concerned to be equally happy, he finds honesty in the act since it saves him, as he believes, from the guilt of denouncing one woman for the sake of the other. However, Lyman sinks in guilt when he confronts Theo in the hospital, who cannot absorb the shock of the sudden revelation. He even admits to his daughter Bessie that his "character's so bad" (43). But the "truth" he ultimately comes up with is the same as he upheld earlier: "We're all ego, kid, ego plus an occasional prayer" (79). If he is still guilty of betrayal, isn't betrayal "the first law of life" (79)? As Lyman further observes, "a man can be faithful to himself or to other people—but not to both" (79). What he has really violated, he tells Theo, is "the law of hypocrisy" (83). At this point, he recalls the roaring, lascivious lion on safari, and the words he flung toward the beast: "We love our lives, you goddam lion! –you and me both!" (99). Lyman acknowledges his wildness but then justifies it as the proof of life in him. He does not believe in the moral law and therefore in self-consistency. An individual, according to him, is "a fourteen-room house," living multiple selves in diverse circumstances (81). To be faithful to each of them is, in Lyman's eyes, self-integrity which is basically incompatible with social morality.

The Ride is "a completely political play," Miller tells Bigsby. Lyman is "the apotheosis of the individualist who has arrived at a point where the rest of the world has faded into insignificance." He is "the quintessential Eighties man.... He...keeps saying he's telling the truth about himself, but in fact he's had to conceal everything" (qtd. in Bigsby, *Modern American Drama* 122). This type of character, Miller further clarifies in another interview, is not new: "it's just that Ronald Reagan gave it the imprimatur of society" (qtd. in Griffin 175). After Vietnam, Watergate, stagflation and energy crises, the American people did not want to hear a Jimmy Carter talking of limits, taxes and sacrifice. Reagan understood the need for a laudatory rhetoric that would restore the nation's faith in its old myths of innocence and success. However, selective perception and denial were fast thinning down the line between appearance and reality. In fact, denials continued throughout Reagan's life: "denying that his tax cuts could be responsible for the mounting federal deficits; denying that his cuts in low-income housing subsidies could be responsible for the rise in homelessness; ...and forgetting virtually everything about the Iran-Contra...scandal" (Shockley 49). Reagan examined the values in hardly any greater depth than Lyman (Lie-man). But he "had been in some measure the Wizard of US," as political analysts have observed, "a fabulist presiding over a wondrous Emerald City of the Mind" (qtd. in Shockley 53). The moral rhetoric both Reagan and Lyman appropriate disguises the moral decay of the "Me" generation, and the play shows how "truth" can be a product of power or a cultural construct.

Paralysis as a metaphor for total inaction in the face of overwhelming forces lies at the heart of *Broken Glass* (1994). Miller got the idea of the story in the thirties, he says, but did not write it until the nineties "when ethnic cleansing [once again] came into the news, and suddenly [the past] became part of the present" (qtd. in

Lewis 6). Set in 1938 Brooklyn, the play alludes to Kristallnacht, the
Night of Broken Glass, when Nazis in Berlin smashed the windows
of Jewish shops and synagogues, desecrated Jewish cemeteries, and
killed about a hundred Jews. Miller's central concern is the *mystery*
of how the story traveled across four thousand miles of water and
crippled Sylvia Gellburg, a housewife in Brooklyn. The task, says
Miller, is to find that juncture where "a public concern and a private
neurosis .... actually meet" (qtd. in Bigsby, "Miller in the Nineties"
180). The paradox is that even people joined by love hardly realize
when they have become strangers to each other. *Broken Glass* shows
the effects of unspoken tyrannies and unacknowledged fears on
personal as well as social level, adding a new dimension to the "What
love ... I know how to kill?" theme of Miller's *After the Fall* (240).

The Gellburgs love each other. But what happens when love cannot
hold against the vain attempts to bypass embarrassing truths? All this
can ultimately become manifest in feelings of worthlessness
accompanied by "an irrational, often righteous fury," directed as
much against self as against others (Lahr 94). Phillip and Sylvia "had
once wounded one another mortally by not seeing what they should
have seen," just as many American Jews had crippled themselves
morally "by not seeing that what was happening on the other side of
the world was the same as if it had been happening on the next block"
(Peter). Sylvia might have had a career if Phillip had not forbidden
her to return to work after the birth of their son. Confining herself to
household chores and reading, she gradually builds up an insular
world which he fails to penetrate. Perhaps because Sylvia sees herself
as a victim of Phillip's apathy (though he does not realize it as such),
she is especially traumatized by the news of Nazi atrocities in
Germany. The news photo of two old men forced to scrub a sidewalk
with toothbrushes is for Sylvia, as for the audience, an image of
appalling humiliation to which she ultimately relates herself, as a Jew
whose fears are little appreciated by her callous society. More
disquieting is the fact that Jews also have their Jews. Sylvia's
equation of her humiliation by Phillip with the Nazi treatment of
German Jews is reflected in the dream she reports to Dr. Hyman:
"They're Germans. . . . And the whole crowd is chasing after me. . .a
man catches me. . .and begins kissing me, and then he starts to cut off
my breast. . . . I think it's Phillip" (110). "Given the mores of that
time and society, and her amenable personality," Miller explains,
"she was not likely to take an independent route, so she turns against

herself" (qtd. in Griffin 186). She cannot accept herself any more than she can accept her husband.

On the other hand, Phillip feels ambiguous about his Jewish identity. At times, he is proud of being the only Jew to have worked for Brooklyn Guarantee; but at others, he is a self-hating Jew who sounds even anti-Semitic. Phillip is a split personality because he cannot fully accept an identity which has come to be seen by most as an aberration. To this public sense of humiliation is added Sylvia's rejection. Sylvia's indifference to Phillip ever since his objection to her work might be a cause for his present impotence. As his powerlessness in the face of anti-Semitism paradoxically makes him less tolerant toward his own community, so does his sexual paralysis turn him against his wife on whom he blames it all. Conversely, when he feels guilty for Sylvia's illness, his failure to get her to walk causes self-loathing. "He knows with one part of his mind" what he is doing to Sylvia, says Miller, "with the other part ... he's denying it" (qtd. in Griffin 185).

The Gellburgs are "both right," and they are "both wrong" (Lahr 95). But what each fails to do is to walk through "the dangerous personal areas of rancor" and meet the other (Lahr 95). The play's climax brings together the private and the public denial in Hyman's speech on mutual persecution: "*Everybody's* persecuted.... It's really amazing—you can't find anybody who's persecuting anybody else" (152). John Lahr calls it "the punishing mysteries of our lives" (96). *Broken Glass* dramatizes the cycle of evasions and denials which shut out from our view the grim reality about us. Politically, it may even take on the form of the Holocaust denial as by Irving. But in *Broken Glass* the real is eventually recovered more confidently than in any other recent plays by Miller.

For all his recognition of the indeterminacy of truth and the unreliability of knowledge, Miller cannot give up his quest for value and meaning. His late plays may question the traditional realist transparency but do not reduce reference to simulacrum. While problematizing his earlier liberal assumptions, they make humanist premises available for reconsideration. Miller says: "I've become less and less interested in making an arraignment and more and more interested in the balance of forces. We're always patching ourselves together; life is a matter of exchanging one half-truth for another. We have to struggle, to absorb, the terrible impact of ambiguity" (qtd. in Allen 36). He goes on to insist, in the manner of Alan Wilde, that we try to create meaning in the face of—not in place of—a meaningless universe (Wilde, *Horizons* 148). In his *Middle Grounds*, Wilde calls it "a revitalised humanism" for "our postmodern age," which, being opposed to the imperialistic/confident humanism/individualism of the past, situates individuals "in a world to which their acts bring value … but not … definitive truth" (108). "To react to the loss of center with despair can only lead to alienation," Susan Abbotson correctly observes, but to acknowledge and accept it, can bring about new and varied forms of bonding (23). The late plays of Miller acknowledge the aporia of *both* the impossibility *and* necessity of a moral life. They strive to recuperate the affirmative in a world that is itself ontologically incomplete and epistemologically problematic.

In *Archbishop*, Sigmund's final resistance—despite all fiction of the state as well as of the self—is sincere. He resolves to remain a rooted artist, as Miller puts it, "rather than the refugee which would menace his artistic life, and therefore make him useless to the future" ("An Interview" 43). Underneath "the passionate uncommitment" which makes truth problematic in *Elegy*, Miller believes, there is "a skeletal structure of human relations" which, though not redeeming, constitutes whatever is real in the play (qtd. in Bigsby, *Modern American Drama* 116). The Man finally learns that a lover has to earn the "satisfaction" of being "cleansed by a whole sorrow" if he is to share the agony of another person (17). In *Love Story*, Tom cannot have any of his conjectures confirmed by his source. But it is his commitment to justice which sustains his investigative spirit in the face of all uncertainty. He wants to believe certain things, though he understands that belief is *not* knowledge. The "pair of survivors" in *I Can't Remember Anything*, however disillusioned, share a sense of loss and depend on each other "for whatever human connection they have" (Weales 184). Moreover, Leo, quite unlike Leonora, finds reality and meaning within the very idea of work, no matter if under the shadow of death. In *Clara*, too, in his daughter's catastrophe Kroll "has rediscovered himself," to quote Miller, "and glimpsed the tragic collapse of values that he finally cannot bring himself to renounce." Kroll's struggle is to keep "faith with the best in himself," Miller adds, even as the moral world grows more fragile (*Timebends* 591). To come to *The Ride*, Lyman's unabashed love of life and his "self-integrity" do not absolve him of his indifference to others. The last scene insists on Lyman's need to *re*-examine his life and "end up [at least] with the right regrets" (29). Lastly, *Broken Glass*, which ends with Sylvia finding her balance as Phillip falls dead, asks how to contain the impulse of denial, and "grasp" the shames and responsibilities of being human" (Peter).

While probing the nature of reality, Miller's late plays often seem to call everything into question. But "there are still structures of what you would call moral view," reasserts the playwright, "which lead us into suffering and death" ("Just Looking" 86). How recuperation is possible under the pressure of unreality, how continuity and connectiveness can be fostered in a fragmented/disordered world, how meaning can be reinscribed in the face of all contingency and chaos—these are the most moving questions posed by the late plays of Miller.

Works Cited

Abbotson, Susan C.W. "Towards a Humanistic Democracy: The Balancing Acts of Arthur Miller and August Wilson." Ph.D. diss., University of Connecticut, 1997.

Allen, Jennifer. "Miller's Tale." *New York* 16 (24 Jan. 1983): 33-37.

Bigsby, Christopher. Afterword to *The Archbishop's Ceiling*, by Arthur Miller. London: Methuen, 1984. 91-95.

———. *A Critical Introduction to Twentieth-Century American Drama*. Vol. 2. Cambridge: Cambridge University Press, 1984.

———. "Miller in the Nineties." In *The Cambridge Companion to Arthur Miller*. Edited by Christopher Bigsby. Cambridge: Cambridge University Press, 1997. 168-83.

———. *Modern American Drama, 1945—1990*. Cambridge: Cambridge University Press, 1992.

Gergen, Kenneth J. *The Saturated Self: Dilemmas of Identity in Contemporary Life*. New York: Basic, 1991.

Griffin, Alice. *Understanding Arthur Miller*. Columbia: University of South Carolina Press, 1996.

Hutcheon, Linda. *A Poetics of Postmodernism*. New York: Routledge, 1988.

Lahr, John. "Dead Souls." *New Yorker* 70 (9 May 1994): 94-96.

Langteau, Paula. Review of *Resurrection Blues*, by Arthur Miller. *The Arthur Miller Society Newsletter* 6 (2002): 4-6.

Lewis, Peter. "Headlines That Unlocked a 50-Year Story." *Sunday Telegraph* 31 July 1994: Review 6.

Lyotard, Jean-Francois and Jean-Loup Thébaud. *Just Gaming*. Translated by Godzich. 1979. Minneapolis: University of Minnesota Press, 1985.

May, Todd. *The Moral Theory of Poststructuralism*. State College: Pennsylvania State University Press, 1995.

Melley, Timothy. "Postmodern Amnesia: Trauma and Forgetting in Tim O'Brien's *In the Lake of the Woods*." *Contemporary Literature* 44.1 (2003): 106-31.

Miller, Arthur. *After the Fall*. In Arthur Miller's Collected Plays. 2 vols. New York: Viking, 1981. 2: 125-242.

———. *The Archbishop's Ceiling*. London: Methuen, 1984.

———. "Author's Note." *Some Kind of Love Story*. New York: Dramatists Play Service, 1983. 3.

———. *Broken Glass*. New York: Penguin, 1994.

———. "A Conversation with Arthur Miller." Interview by Jan Balakian. *Michigan Quarterly Review* 29.2 (1990): 158-71.

———. *Clara*. In *Danger: Memory!* New York: Grove, 1986.

———. *Elegy for a Lady*. New York: Dramatists Play Service, 1982.

———. *I Can't Remember Anything*. In *Danger: Memory!* New York: Grove, 1986.

———. "An Interview with Arthur Mller." By Jan Balakian. *Studies in American Drama 1945 – Present* 6.1 (1991): 29-47.

———. Introduction to *The Archbishop's Ceiling; The American Clock: Two Plays*. New York: Grove, 1989.

———. " 'Just Looking for a Home': A Conversation with Arthur Miller." Interview by Steven R. Centola. *American Drama* 1.1 (1991): 85-94.

———. "The Last Yankee: An Interview with Arthur Miller." By Steven R. Centola. *American Drama* 5.1 (1995): 78-98.

———. *The Ride Down Mount Morgan*. New York: Penguin, 1991.

———. *Some Kind of Love Story*. New York: Dramatists Play Service, 1983.

———. *Timebends: A Life*. New York: Grove, 1987.

Otten, Terry. *The Temptation of Innocence in the Dramas of Arthur Miller*. Columbia: University of Missouri Press, 2002.

Peter, John. "A Raw Slice of Humanity." *Sunday Times* 14 Aug. 1994: Features.

Rich, Frank. "Arthur Miller's *Danger: Memory!*" *New York Times* 9 Feb. 1987: C15.

Royal National Theatre. *Platform Papers: 7. Arthur Miller*. London: Royal National Theatre, 1995.

Schlueter, June. "Miller in the Eighties." In *The Cambridge Companion to Arthur Miller*. Edited by Christopher Bigsby. Cambridge: Cambridge University Press, 1997. 152-67.

Schlueter, June and James K. Flanagan. *Arthur Miller*. New York: Ungar, 1987.

Shockley, John S. "*Death of a Salesman* and American Leadership: Life Imitates Art". *Journal of American Culture* 17 (1994): 49-56.

Weales, Gerald. "A Pair of Survivors: Miller's *Danger: Memory!*" *Commonweal* (27 Mar. 1987): 184-85.

Wilde, Alan. *Horizons of Assent: Modernism, Postmodernism and the Ironic Imagination*. Baltimore: Johns Hopkins University Press, 1981.

———. *Middle Grounds: Studies in Contemporary American Fiction*. Philadelphia: University of Philadelphia Press, 1987.

The Dangers of Memory
in Arthur Miller's
I Can't Remember Anything

Susan C. W. Abbotson

I Can't Remember Anything is one of the two short plays which
make up the program Arthur Miller entitled *Danger: Memory*! In the
play Leonora pays one of her regular visits to her old friend Leo. The
two of them discuss the state of their current lives and recall what it
was like before Leonora's husband, Frederick, died. Unable to
reconcile their own different outlooks on life, they quarrel and
Leonora leaves. The play may be "thin," but, as Terry Otten points
out, the text is "by no means simple" (190), and a reading of the play
is further complicated by the existence of two versions, one published
by Grove in 1986, and another by the Dramatists Play Service in
1987. This reading is based on the later of the published texts, which
offers a substantially different ending.

I Can't deals with that perennial Miller concern, the necessity for
people to acknowledge their past as an active part of their current
existence. Nothing can be more important to our placing of the past in
our lives than the concept of memory, but as Miller recognizes,
memory holds many dangers, some of which he attempts to illustrate
in *I Can't*, which (ironically, given its title), shows the dangers of
overindulging in memories of the past.

The past, when properly viewed, provides a comforting sense of
continuity and connection. Patricia Schroeder rightly points out how,
in Miller's plays, "the past is always a crucial defining element of the
present" (76). In *I Can't*, Leo and Leonora are encouraged to
remember everything they have been in the past, to help them to

define who they are in the present. Leo and Leonora find a comfort in their routine companionship, but this is suddenly destroyed when Leo chooses to change their relationship. His motivation lies buried in his refusal to accept the real past and his preference for a fake past he has created in his imagination; this selfish decision hurts both himself and his old friend Leonora.

A sense of mystery pervades the start of *I Can't,* and audiences are forced to ask numerous questions. Central among these are: what makes Leo such a recluse, and why is Leonora so patently self-destructive? The answer, we come to learn, is not the world that they both try to blame, but themselves and their own flawed natures. Both construct the present in which they must live through the way they perceive the past. Neither offers an ideal way to live, as both have difficulty dealing with the role of the past in their lives and accepting any real responsibility for their own lives.[1] Both Leo and Leonora are reclusive to the point of danger. Since the death of Frederick, who seems to have acted as a catalyst of connection to them both, both have lost touch with the society around them, and neither improves on this condition by the close of the play. The play shows how our minds have the power to shape reality and define the identity of the self.

Contradictions and ambivalences permeate the entire play. For example, the setting of the play in Leo's kitchen evokes an island apart from the rest of the world. Leo lives the life of a recluse out on a country back road, out of the way of the larger society. The line drawings of dead friends which adorn his kitchen serve as a constant reminder to him of his past, but also of his bleak future, as their deceased status indicates the similar death that awaits him. Leo will not let the past be destroyed and hangs onto it tenaciously, patching up old objects so as to maintain their presence, though on the surface allowing people to think that this is merely his resistance to modern commercialism. But while on the one hand he surrounds himself with his (idealized) past and seems to withdraw into it, on the other hand he is fighting to remain a part of the world. Both Leo and Leonora are consistently torn between such opposites.

Leo has been described as a man living in "good faith [with] no illusions about life," a person who is unafraid to "accept his past" (Centola 137). Though this is certainly the impression Leo likes to convey, it really is not true. Leo's whole life is an illusion, based on an idealized past from which he cannot progress. As Gerald Weales indicates, Leo is obsessed with his "roseate view of the years in which [Frederick], his partner, was the center of their existence" (184). He will not allow anything, finally, to tamper with his whitewashed memory of Frederick. When Leonora shows an unwillingness to continue indulging in such memories he grows increasingly upset with her. Centola sees Leo's life as "meaningful because he has made it so with his altruistic behavior" (137). But what if that altruistic behavior is shown to be a sham, as it is in the revised version of the play?

Leo has been nice to Leonora purely out of selfish motives, to try and maintain a link, through her, to his dead friend and leader. Now that she is refusing to play the game, by refusing to remember, he attempts to cast her off as an unnecessary burden, telling her she means "absolutely nothing" to him (26), despite her evident need for his company to maintain her own sanity. Marilyn Stasio recognizes that Leonora may not be as irresponsible as some critics have seen her, and that fault can be found with Leo. She points out that he "is crotchety because his vague companion has forgotten all the ritual signposts—the old friendships and the shared anecdotes of two long lifetimes—that have made their companionship comfortable and secure" (346). Meanwhile, Leonora, "is bewildered by the way he clings to the familiar rituals and safe past, refusing to acknowledge what really matters: the eroded quality of their present lives" (346). Unlike Leo, Leonora desires to improve her present life rather than spend the remainder of it hiding in the past, a past which we discover was not so perfect. Despite Leo's commendations of Frederick, in reality he was a coarse, loud-mouthed, and unfaithful individual.

Leo is not in the best of health, evidently suffering from arthritis and exuding the feeling that he is just filling in time before his death. What Otten views as Leo's "active participation in life," (201) underscored by his constant stage business, seems more an active participation in death. Leo is unhealthily obsessed with death and dying. He argues with Leonora over which of them will die first, and surrounds himself with images of death. In many ways this is because that is what the past has become for him, an arena of death. What he needs is a more positive way of dealing with the past which will allow him, instead, to concentrate on life—which can then allow him a future. He tries to do this, by centering his remembrances on images of food and parties, but he knows in his heart that this time has passed; he no longer has Frederick to follow, and he feels lost in the modern world. We are given as Leo's key quality the fact that he is "stubborn," and it is clear that he has not yet entirely given in to this death impulse. This manifests itself largely through his connection to Leonora, despite his attempts by the close of the play to sever that connection.

The similarity between the characters' names, Leo and Leonora, suggests that she may be another version of Leo, and she is. Leonora provides both a contrast and a complement to Leo. Where he is small and sickly, she is as large and colorful as her wrap, evoking a life she would like to deny but cannot escape. Where Leo wants to immerse himself in his past, but is beginning, reluctantly, to forget certain details,[2] Leonora pretends to remember nothing, though the memories insist upon imposing themselves. She declares that she hates crosswords because they are so trivial, but she really hates them because they force you to remember things. Extremes, as ever, are bad, and it will be a balance between these two which will offer us the best way to live our lives. Otten suggests that "they depend on each other for mutual support" (200), and it is ultimately only through their connection to each other that these two will survive, as alone, each runs the evident (and ultimately selfish) danger of totally withdrawing from life—Leo into his past and Leonora into oblivion.

Leonora recognizes her connection to Leo and may believe that through this connection she can reconnect to others or with hope itself. She insists that Leo always sees the purpose in things because this is what she herself so desperately needs to do. She displaces her belief onto her closest friend so she can remain close without having to feel that it may betray her. Leo, although a recluse, does resist his impulse to cut himself off from life—evidenced in his continuation of hope (despite having recognized and refused to ignore evil in the world). Also, his decision to leave his organs to the hospital may reaffirm his morbid fascination with his own impending death, but it is also an act of attrition, fellowship, involvement, and connection, which seems to counter his current isolation—although he is giving the organs for research work rather than as a donor. But Leo's explanation that since the world is only a mass of chemicals, it need not be judged by human standards, is less true optimism than a denial of humanity. He needs to maintain connections to his present as well as his past, in order to remind him continually of both his own and others' humanity; part of this may lead to painful realizations, but such pain will remind him that human beings have feelings and are more than chemicals. It is only through this more embracing recognition that his optimism can be honest, just as Leonora's memories will only be honest when they embrace both the past and the present as worthy of her involvement.

While Leonora, in her despair, is drawn to Leo's apparent optimism, he is drawn, in his sickliness, to her life-force. Their connection to each other keeps them both on the side of life. He forces her to remember (even as she goads him into remembering for her). She forces him to hope (even as, or partly because, she tries to argue him out of his optimism). For a time they sustain each other. Leonora's memories assist Leo in remembering, as he begins, unwillingly, to forget; Leo's hope assists Leonora in refusing to finally give in to the despair she has been struggling against. John Beaufort is quite right to point towards the "depth and constancy of the old friends' interdependence and mutual support" (347), but he ignores the fact that Miller also displays the depth of their mutual betrayals. Despite their connection, neither can consistently supply what each so desperately needs, as both withdraw from that connection when it becomes too complicated.

Behind the apparently secure seclusion that surrounds them, Leo and Leonora are filled with uncertainty and discontent. For Leo, the past is not enough, and for Leonora, the present fails to satisfy. We hear Leonora cough and swallow as she enters to hint at her suppressed discomfort, and both of them seem tense and quarrelsome throughout the play. Both are under an inordinate amount of strain as they try to make their lives more comfortable by pursuing the wrong goals. What each needs to learn is that the past is neither a refuge nor a curse, but an aid towards ensuring a healthy present and future. The present and future cannot be avoided, but should be embraced with strength and understanding, which the proper acknowledgment of the past can provide.

Leonora drinks too much, a classic symbol of avoidance, but what is she avoiding? She is attempting to avoid her own life. Telling us she can no longer even taste food, we get a sense of her cutting herself off from physical sensations in her attempt to withdraw. When Leo reminds her of eating bread the week before—symbolically the staff of life—her self-imposed forgetfulness dissipates a little and she starts to remember. Her memories are of her past life and are thus a reminder of life itself, just as they are a part of her current one. It seems that Leonora is unhappy less from her apparent loss of memory, but more from her inability to forget entirely. The point is, she does remember, despite her attempts not to do so. Initially this evidences itself as she recalls trivial things like the dentist, the plumber and the raccoon. But she continues to suppress the more personal aspects of her life, as if she is trying to eradicate herself, by eradicating her past. We should ask why she does this.

Both characters' connection to the past is suspect, as in the past both have been self-admitted heavy-drinkers, which may have led them to a rather distorted vision of the world, or even led them to have no vision at all. Both admit that they drank their way through that defining event of the twentieth century, World War Two, and largely by-passed its concerns. Thus, they also missed the Holocaust, that twentieth century specter of evil. It is, in part, that specter towards which they are now so ambivalent—recognizing its inevitable impact on the world, yet also wishing to escape from under its shadow. They feel trapped by it, partly because it lies, as yet, unacknowledged in their forgotten past, and so continually threatens to reemerge and destroy their potential future—possibly, in the form of death itself.

Leonora does not want to hear any current, outside news, because she can no longer cope with its potential horrors. She says that she wants to die because she feels so useless and unnecessary. Leo and Leonora have evidently been meeting like this on an escalating basis for the last ten years—giving Leonora, in particular, the sense of structure in her life which she needed after her husband's death. But now, Leonora is consciously trying not to remember anything in order to make her life seem "imaginary" and fictional (in a sense, utterly unstructured, she is offering herself to the chaos, as an act not of courage but more of self-immolation), for such lives are easier to live as they do not require the same level of involvement. Memory insists upon involvement, and involvement can be dangerous as it forces one to face up to responsibilities which Leonora appears to be seeking to avoid. To recall is as hard, at times, as it is dangerous—but it is also necessary. Beaufort sees Leonora as "a disillusioned idealist" (347), and Centola describes her as "a portrait of despair. . .a woman who has lost all hope and finds no meaning in life. . .her despondence colors her perspective of everything else and even causes her to view America as a society in decline" (137). When one starts to see life as meaningless, then the past also loses its meaning—as it does for Leonora. Leonora has tried to eradicate her relationship with the past, for memory insists on involvement of a kind which scares her, but such involvement is necessary to fully live and should not be avoided. And Leonora is not just fighting the past but also the present and future: she is scared of what will become of her. Leonora has seen the evil around her, despaired at her ability to make a difference, and given up the fight.

Leonora recreates the past into something brighter than the present. She pictures it as a period when she had no real responsibilities. She tries to convince herself, and Leo, that pre-World War Two was a better time—of greater hope, belief, caring, even humanity—but, in truth, the war did not change things, only bring them out into the open for those who were willing to take note: evil has always been in the world; it had just been easier to ignore before such events as the Holocaust occurred. Leo offers us evidence that their past had not been so wonderful in his description of his father dying drunk and alone in the mines. Leonora must face the fact that she was content in the past only because she had severely restricted her view of the world—just as she stayed with her husband despite all his affairs, by ignoring them. She can no longer live with such self-imposed limits, as the world insists that she view it fully.

The picture we are given of Frederick, Leonora's dead husband, ironically, brims with life: both in his connection to food (bread and salami), and sexuality (making lascivious jokes and sleeping with many women). In trying to forget him, Leonora is separating herself off from a potential source of life. Of course, she is also separating herself from a potential source of pain, which is why she has buried his memory. But to live a full life necessitates some pain. Leo forces her to remember, and it is necessary that she does. Frederick had, symbolically, built bridges for a living and for the living; with his death, it has been hard for both Leo and Leonora to maintain such connections/bridges or build further ones, but this, also, is necessary.

The ability to look to the past and see it in its entirety is what assists us in finding a footing in the present; there will always be danger in concentrating too much on either the bad or the good. For a firm footing, balance is the key. Once Leonora renews her connection to the past she has tried to eradicate, she may draw strength from it as well as warning. The "samba" record that her son has sent, allows Leonora and Leo to recall something vital from their past which may help sustain them into the future—not death or betrayal, but a moment of joy and the comradeship of dance. Together, they do an old-fashioned samba to the record, and are strengthened by this moment of close connection; they even flirt a little to show the sexual vibrancy (life-force) that the dance has awakened in them (although this is soon shattered by Leo's banishment of Leonora at the close of the play).

Lawrence, Leonora's son, is related to these two in ways beyond his blood-ties and initials: he too appears to have been searching for some kind of hope in a disappointing world. He has headed to an Eastern retreat and tried to find contentment in Buddhist philosophy. He may even be finding some direction, as he is now reconnecting with his mother after three years of silence. He sends her a record, and this time one to which his mother can actually relate. Due to his youth he has been able to conduct his search more openly and with greater vigor. He is also less experienced and less likely to be discouraged by past failures. Leo and Leonora have a greater struggle due to their age. Leonora is, at least, in her seventies, and Leo in his sixties.[3] Living in the youth culture of America, to prove themselves still vital at such an age is bound to take even greater effort, but it is, nevertheless, something they should continue to attempt.

Centola insists that *I Can't* moves toward an epiphany and a positive outcome for the characters involved. While this is certainly true of its companion play, *Clara*, it does not apply so clearly to Leo and Leonora. June Schleuter's description of the play as "autumnal," and "poignant," coupled with her observation that the players' conversation is "settling always on the decay of American life" (163), suggests a less optimistic reading of the play. Leo and Leonora may strive for life but will not escape lonely deaths. Admittedly, their failure is more apparent in the later edition of the play, and Centola bases his assessment on the earlier version, in which it is not so evident. The major difference between the two versions of the play is that the later version includes a major argument between Leo and Leonora. The disagreement begins with Leo asking Leonora not to come round every day as he declares that she is making his health suffer. She leaves in umbrage, and he seems elated that he has finally curtailed their friendship, stating that he has never cared for Leonora, but only her deceased husband, Frederick: "Don't you know there's nothing between us?—I did it for him, that's all....You're nothing to me" (26). This assures our realization that Leo has as many hang-ups and faults as Leonora and is certainly not the ideal some critics have described.

Centola views Leo as a "model of human conduct" in his ability to face "life's absurdities (aging and death most noticeably) with courage and the determination not to be defeated in his struggle to give it meaning" which he does, Centola insists, "by accepting the freedom and responsibility that every person has to make the most of their lives" (138). Such an assessment becomes decidedly uncertain given Miller's revised ending. While Weales suggests that Leo and Leonora are "a pair of survivors who depend on one another for whatever human connection they have" (184), in the end, that connection is broken, and largely through Leo's selfishness. It is Leo's insistence on his false memories which destroys both their friendship, and any chance that either one will be able to re-engage in a meaningful life.

Notes

[1] In *Timebends*, Miller tells us that he based Leo and Leonora on his old friends Sandy and Louisa Calder—both heavy drinkers who felt as if they had come from a previous era and so felt somewhat cut off from the present. They lived lives of "bohemian acceptance, judging no-one, curious about everything, but not far beneath the surface was a stubborn and somehow noble sense of responsibility for the country, a sure instinct for decency that, in the wildly experimental and super self-indulgent sixties, seemed in its quality of unpretentious simplicity all but lost to history," and he intended for *I Can't* to be an expression of his "love for them both" (503). However, Leo and Leonora take on a life of their own which moves them away from Miller's original intention: although they share similar traits, they are not, finally, as responsible as the Calders.

[2] Leo is growing forgetful, and it is against his will. He forgets little details here and there, such as laying the table and who it was who called him earlier that day, and he is frustrated with his inability to calculate numbers as he has in the past.

[3] Though Miller does not tell us their ages directly, these ages are appropriate given that Leonora probably married in her late teens or early twenties, was married for 45 years, has been a widow for ten, and is 12 years older than Leo.

Works Cited

Beaufort, John. "Memories Infuse Two Miller One-Acters." *Christian Science Monitor* 11 Feb 1987. In *New York Theatre Critics' Review* 48 (1987): 347.

Centola, Steven R., ed. *The Achievement of Arthur Miller: New Essays.* Dallas: Contemporary Research, 1995.

Miller, Arthur. *I Can't Remember Anything.* In *Danger: Memory!* New York: Dramatists Play Service, 1987.

———. *Timebends: A Life.* New York: Grove, 1987.

Otten, Terry. *The Temptation of Innocence in the Dramas of Arthur Miller.* Columbia: University of Missouri Press, 2002.

Schleuter, June. "Miller in the Eighties." In *The Cambridge Companion to Arthur Miller.* Edited by Christopher Bigsby. Cambridge: Cambridge University Press, 1997: 152-67.

Schroeder, Patricia R. *The Presence of the Past in Modern American Drama.* Cranbury, NJ: Associated University Press, 1989.

Stasio, Marilyn. "Miller at Grips with Memory." *New York Post* 9
     Feb. 1987. In *New York Theatre Critics' Review* 48 (1987): 346.
Weales, Gerald. "A Pair of Survivors: Miller's *Danger: Memory!*"
     Commonweal 114 (27 Mar. 1987): 184-85.

Notes to Preface

Bigsby, Christopher. "Biographical Notes." and "Introduction to the Revised Edition" *The Portable Arthur Miller.* Edited by Christopher Bigsby. New York: Penguin, 1995.

Billington, Michael. "The Guardian." *Arthur Miller and Company.* Edited by Christopher Bigsby. London: Methuen, 1990. 187-89.

Clurman, Harold. "Biographical Notes," *The Portable Arthur Miller.* Edited by Harold Clurman. New York: Penguin, 1971. vii-x.

Otten, Terry. *The Temptation of Innocence in the Dramas of Arthur Miller.* Columbia: The University of Missouri Press, 2002.

Index

Note: Entries for Arthur Miller are not listed fully in the index.

Playing for Time, 16-17, 19, 21-
24, 27
Auschwitz, 21
Bergen-Belsen, 21
Characters:
Alma, 23
Elzvieta, 23
Etalina, 22
Fania Fénelon, 19, 21-23,
27
Marianne, 22
Pontius Pilate, 25
Poor Richard's Almanac
(Franklin), 55
Pradhan, N. S., 72
Price, The, 42, 47-49, 52, 72, 74,
76
Characters:
Esther Franz, 48
Solomon, 48, 52, 76
Victor Franz, 47-49, 71-72,
74, 76-77
Walter Franz, 42, 47-49, 52,
74, 76
Puritan, Puritanism, 3, 17, 21, 24,
80-82
Pynchon, Thomas, 5

Reagan, Ronald, 108, 114, 117
Redgrave, Vanessa, 21
Reilly, Peter, 112
Resurrection Blues, 19
Rich, Frank, 113-14
Richelieu, Cardinal (*The Three
Musketeers*), 102
Ricoeur, Paul, 16
Ride Down Mt. Morgan, 41, 52,
56, 64-65, 107, 115-17, 120
Characters:
Bessie, 116
Leah, 116
Lyman Felt, 52, 58, 65,
116-17, 120
Nurse Logan, 65

Theo, 116-17
Tom Wilson, 41, 65
Rinehart, Mrs., 103
Roth, Martin, 46
Roudané, Matthew, 8-10
Royal National Theatre, 107-108

Saint Augustine, 27
Santayana, George, 15
Savran, David, 31, 37
Schlueter, June, 65, 110-11, 132
Schneider, Daniel E., 102
Schweizer, Karl W., 101-102,
104-105
Schroeder, Patricia, 125
Sengupta, Ashis, 107-123
Shepard, Sam, 5
Shockley, John S., 117
Slattery, Mary Grace (1st wife),
56-59, 61
Smith, Adam, 22-23
Smith, William, xi, 79-97
Snyder, Albert, 100, 102-103,
105
Snyder, Lorraine, 105
Snyder, Ruth, 100-103, 105
Solzhenitsyn, Alexander, 108
Some Kind of Love Story, 111-14,
120
Characters:
Angela, 112-13
Felix, 112
Tom, 112-14, 120
Stasio, Marilyn, 127
Straton, Doctor, 103
Sunday, Billy, 103

Testament of Dr. Mabuse, 104
Thanatos, 21-22
Thoreau, Henry David, 4
Three Musketeers, The, 102
Time Magazine, 34

Contributors

SUSAN C. W. ABBOTSON is Assistant Professor in Modern and Contemporary Drama at Rhode Island College. She has published extensively on Arthur Miller, including *Understanding Death of a Salesman* (with Brenda Murphy), and *The Student Companion to Arthur Miller*. Her most recent book was *Masterpieces of Twentieth Century American Drama* (2005) for Greenwood Press, and her *Critical Companion to Arthur Miller*, an encyclopedic reference guide to the playwright, is due to be published Fall 2007 by Facts on File.

FRANK BERGMANN is Professor of English and German at Utica College. He has published books on John William De Forest and Robert Grant and has edited *Upstate Literature*, a volume of essays on the literature of upstate New York. In 1973 he published an essay on Miller (in German, with emphasis on *Incident at Vichy*) in the handbook *Amerikanische Literatur der Gegenwart*, and in 1996 he hosted the 3rd International Arthur Miller Conference at Utica. He is a member of the Arthur Miller Society and has written reviews for its newsletter.

CARLOS CAMPO teaches English and Drama at the Community College of Southern Nevada in Las Vegas, where he is the Dean of Arts & Letters. He has written extensively on Arthur Miller, and has been published in *English Language Notes* and the *Film/Literature Quarterly*. He is also a former Arthur Miller Society Vice President.

GEORGE P. CASTELLITO is Professor of Modern American Literature at Felician College in New Jersey and is presently serving as curator of the A.R. Ammons collection housed as the college. He has published articles on Miller, Stevens, Ginsberg, and Williams.

STEVEN R. CENTOLA is Professor of English at Millersville University in Pennsylvania and founding President of the Arthur Miller Society. As well as publishing his own critical work on Miller and several interviews with the playwright in various scholarly journals, he has also edited numerous volumes on Miller, including *The Theater Essays of Arthur Miller* (1996) and *Echoes Down the Corridor* (2000), which he collaborated on with the playwright. With

Michelle Cirulli, he edited *The Critical Response to Arthur Miller (2006),* and his last interview with Miller will be published in the Winter 2007 issue of the *Michigan Quarterly Review.*

PAULA T. LANGTEAU is Campus Dean of the University of Wisconsin – Marinette. Her essay, "Miller's *Salesman*: An Early Vision of Absurdist Theatre" was published in *The Achievement of Arthur Miller: New Essays,* and she has written numerous articles and reviews for *The Arthur Miller Society Newsletter.* In 2003, she hosted the 8th International Arthur Miller Conference. The founding Vice President and former President of the Arthur Miller Society, she now serves on the Executive Board.

LEWIS LIVESAY has been at Saint Peter's College for two decades, teaching composition and literature in a New Jersey program named the Educational Opportunity Fund. The E.O.F. Program at Saint Peter's has earned a reputation for its graduation rate and success with developing many non-traditional students into honor students. In November 2006, he published a book essay entitled "Kafka's *The Metamorphosis*: Gregor's Da-sein Paralyzed by Debt" in *Temporality in Life As Seen Through Literature: Contributions to Phenomenology of Life.* In 2005–2006, Lew served his colleagues in the Arthur Miller Society as president.

STEPHEN A. MARINO teaches at Saint Francis College in Brooklyn, New York. His work on Arthur Miller has appeared in *Modern Drama, The Journal of Imagism,* and *The South Atlantic Review.* He is the editor of *"The Salesman Has a Birthday": Essays Celebrating the Fiftieth Anniversary of Arthur Miller's Death of a Salesman* (University Press of America, 2000) and the author of *A Language Study of Arthur Miller's Plays, The Poetic in the Colloquial* (Edwin Mellen Press, 2002). He is the editor of *The Arthur Miller Journal.*

ASHIS SENGUPTA is Reader in English at the University of North Bengal (India). Recipient of the Olive I Reddick Award (1995) and fellow at the Fulbright American Studies Institute in New York (2002), he has published dozens of articles on modern American and Indian English drama in journals/edited volumes of international repute. Sengupta has presented papers at a number of seminars and conferences in India and abroad. He also writes for a leading Indian newspaper. He is currently teaching at the Department of English, Rhode Island College, as a visiting Fulbright Professor.

WILLIAM SMITH teaches English at Red Bank Regional High School in New Jersey, where he is Supervisor of English and Media Services. He has a Master of Arts from Drew University and worked on Miller for his dissertation.